What Do We Need Men For?

What Do We Need Men For?

A Modest Proposal

E. Jean Carroll

St. Martin's Press
New York

With the delicate feelings I am so celebrated for among my friends, I have changed some names here and a few identifying details to preserve the anonymity of certain persons in the book. All events described herein are to the best of my recollection or are drawn from my diaries and videotaped interviews.

First published in the United States by St. Martin's Press, an imprint of St. Martin's Publishing Group.

WHAT DO WE NEED MEN FOR? Copyright © 2019 by E. Jean Carroll. All rights reserved. Printed in the United States of America. For information, address St. Martin's Publishing Group, 120 Broadway, New York, NY 10271.

www.stmartins.com

Letters to "Ask E. Jean" appeared in *Elle* magazine and are reprinted here by the delightful permission of the Hearst Corporation.

Designed by Susan Walsh

Library of Congress Cataloging-in-Publication Data
Names: Carroll, E. Jean, author.
Title: What do we need men for?: a modest proposal / E. Jean Carroll.
Description: First edition. | New York: St. Martin's Press, 2019.
Identifiers: LCCN 2019005307| ISBN 9781250215437 (hardcover) | ISBN 9781250215444 (ebook)
Subjects: LCSH: Men—Humor. | Man-woman relationships—Humor.
Classification: LCC PN6231.M45 .C37 2019 | DDC 818/.602—dc23
LC record available at https://lccn.loc.gov/2019005307

ISBN 978-1-250-21543-7 (hardcover)
ISBN 978-1-250-21544-4 (ebook)

Our books may be purchased in bulk for promotional, educational, or business use. Please contact your local bookseller or the Macmillan Corporate and Premium Sales Department at 1-800-221-7945, extension 5442, or by email at MacmillanSpecialMarkets@macmillan.com.

First Edition: July 2019

10 9 8 7 6 5 4 3 2

To
Lisa Birnbach, Marilyn Johnson, and
Carol Martin with affection and admiration

Men! You're dying to get your hands on this book.
You are excited and a little frightened to read it. Of course!
But first, before enjoying one of the greatest pleasures
known to man (i.e., the reading of *What Do We Need Men For?*),
you must receive a woman's stamp of approval.*

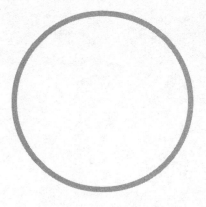

---

* That is, if you actually *know* any women who will vouch for you, which in many cases
is highly doubtful, the stamp goes above.

Contents

I have been assured by a very knowing American of my acquaintance in London, that a young healthy child well nursed, is, at a year old, a most delicious nourishing and wholesome food, whether stewed, roasted, baked, or boiled; and I make no doubt that it will equally serve in a fricassee, or a ragout.

—JONATHAN SWIFT

Prologue

Women! You are fabulous! But for twenty-five years, you have been writing to me at the Ask E. Jean column in *Elle* seeking advice, and for twenty-five years, no matter what problems are driving you crazy—your careers, your wardrobes, your love affairs, your religion, your children, your orgasms, your finances—there comes a line in almost every letter when the cause of your quagmires is revealed. And that cause is *men*.

Ladies, I have been thinking about this dilemma.

It occurs to me that when men are not passing the Ask E. Jean correspondents over for promotion, they are pestering, groping, pawing, pinching, mauling, and underpaying the Ask E. Jean correspondents. But my concern is not confined to Ask E. Jean letter-writers only. The whole female sex seems to agree that men are becoming a nuisance with their lying, cheating, robbing, perjuring, assaulting, murdering, voting debauchers onto the Supreme Court, threatening one another with intercontinental ballistic nuclear warheads, and so on.

Now, I have weighed the two schemes put forth to solve this problem: arresting the chaps and/or impeaching them. Bah! These measures will accomplish nothing!

My scheme does away with the lads entirely. I do, therefore, humbly offer for your consideration the following Modest Proposal:

The average American man is five foot nine and weighs 195.5 pounds. I have been assured by female scientists that the male body is roughly composed of 0.00004 percent iodine, 0.00004 percent iron, 0.05 percent magnesium, 0.15 percent chlorine, 0.15 percent sodium, 0.25 percent sulfur, 0.35 percent potassium, 1 percent phosphorus, 1.5 percent calcium, 3.2 percent nitrogen, 10 percent hydrogen, 18 percent carbon, and 65 percent oxygen, and these elements would, on the open market, fetch around $1 per bloke. If we plump the lads up, we could be looking at $1.02 or $1.03!

The number of males in America is generally reckoned at 164,628,232. Ladies, I propose that we dispose of our chaps at the $1.03 price and put their elements to better use. Not only would this solve all the problems of the Ask E. Jean correspondents, but since ninety-nine out of a hundred calamities throughout history have been caused by men, and since we will be eliminating a prodigious number of idiots, dickweeds, numbskulls, brutes, weaklings, and dingbats (and that's just from the US Congress), the benefit to the nation would be infinite. Plus, with the $170 or $180 million we receive, we will be able to purchase, in return, eleven or twelve genuine Birkin bags.

But before I feel completely satisfied with offering this plan for your consideration, Ladies, and to make absolutely certain that before we sell their elements on the open market, the chaps aren't actually *needed* for anything, I will leave my little cabin in the woods and travel to towns named after women. And when I arrive in each town named after a woman, I will get out of the car and ask people, "What Do We Need Men For?"

Indeed, I plan to leave my little home, which is on an island the size of a mattress eight miles south of Mount Eve in New York, and hit every town named after a woman between Tallulah, Louisiana, and Eden, Vermont *(Eden* is the #131 most popular name for girls in America so far this year, according to BabyCenter.com. *Tallulah,* alas, has recently plunged 581 points in popularity to #2,245).*

I will be driving the spiteful Miss Bingley, my nine-year-old Prius, named after Jane Austen's mean girl in *Pride and Prejudice;* and to keep myself sharp, I will only eat in cafés named after women, listen to music sung by women, drink wines named for-

---

* The popularity of the names fluctuates with births day by day.

women, read books written by women, and wear clothes designed by women. If I eat a burrito in my motel room, it will be
an Amy's organic hand-wrapped, cheddar cheese-, bean-, and
rice-with-Mexican-sauce bitchin' burrito.

Ladies, the time has come. The date is October 6, 2017. Prepare for immortality! The maps, the wine, the books, the clothes,
the Baby Ruths, the Girl Scout cookies are packed. I have said
farewell to the cat, Vagina T. Fireball. The dog, Lewis Carroll,
has taken up his position in the back seat with his head out the
window. I have donned my Korean driving cap, which, to look
fashionable, must be worn pulled down over one eyebrow. To
look *fabulous*, it must cover the entire eye, socket and all, plus half
the other eye. It was designed by a woman who must have had a
chauffeur. I have returned to the cabin to say farewell again, to
the cat. Oh, and one more thing.

As I will be asking people "What Do We Need Men For?" in
the fond hope of getting rid of the male sex forever, I will no
doubt be reminded of certain men in my own life. And though I
am as sweet and gentle as the day I made my first communion, as
seen here:

I will be keeping a list. This list will be called **The Most Hideous Men of My Life List.** I don't know yet which of the foul harassers, molesters, traducers, swindlers, stranglers, and no-goods will make the list, but, Ladies! I warn you. Bad fellows have done bad things to your advice columnist.

This will not be pleasant for you to read. I am sorry. But if we all just lean over and put our heads between our knees, the horrid fainting feeling will pass. No one need be carried from the room.

For instance, when we get to the section of the book about the president and how he throws me against a wall and yanks down my tights in Bergdorf's—do not be alarmed, Ladies. As I write, he is still married to the First Lady.

Anyway, I assure you that I have been attacked by far, far better men than the president. One of my husbands, the glamorous ABC anchorman, for instance, was a famous choker whom I wore for three seasons. Here we all are in a photo taken at a party.

But, happily, not every man we meet will try to yank down my tights—though, in the very first chapter, there *is* a boy who knocks me to the ground and, well, let's not get ahead of ourselves—it takes more than a bunch of dolts to stop your advice columnist! So, Ladies, honk your horns! We've got a big, *big* road trip ahead of us! LET'S GO!

P.S. Let me assure you that I have not the least personal interest in endeavoring to promote this Modest Proposal. I have no men by which I can get a single penny when we sell their elements—no current husbands, bosses, etc., etc.—even if the chaps turn out to fetch prices as high as \$1.05 or \$1.06! I have no other motive than the public good of the nation.

I

"I'm Nothing but Your Punching Bag and Slave."

Elnora, Indiana
(#4,730 Most Popular Girl's Name)

The following are the opinions (ranked in popularity) offered by the men of Gnaw Bone, Indiana, concerning the suspicious fluid Miss Bingley, the Prius, is seeping in a long stream that runs down the Brown County IGA parking lot. It is . . .

1. Oil
2. Antifreeze
3. Brake fluid
4. Windshield wiper liquid
5. Transmission fluid

As I have lived among the male sex of Indiana long enough to form a judgment about their intelligence, I close the car door and put my bag on the asphalt. I know how you love bags, Ladies. Here is my bag.

Eat your heart out, Jane Birkin!

This excellent bag, given to me by the writer Melanie Rock, may come in handy when I am being chased out of towns named after women and required to pack in a hurry. So much handier than Joan Didion's method of typing up and taping her packing list to the inside of her closet door, *viz* in *The White Album:* "2 skirts, 2 jerseys or leotards, 1 pullover sweater, 2 pair shoes, stockings, bra, nightgown, robe, slippers, cigarettes, bourbon,

bag with shampoo, toothbrush and paste, Basis soap, razor, de-
odorant, aspirin, prescriptions, Tampax, face cream, powder,
baby oil."

I, however, do not *need* to type up anything. I simply glance
at the inside flap of my bag . . .

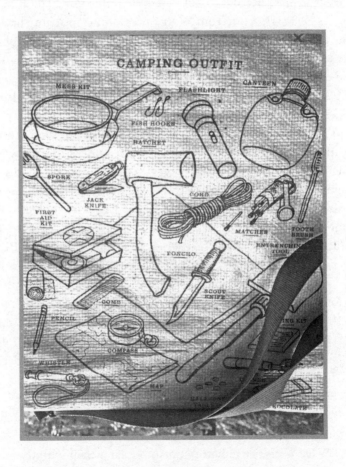

. . . to remember to pack my toothbrush and hatchet. Now, back in the IGA parking lot.

"I'll just take a look at what that fluid can be," I say to the Gnaw-Boners.

I bend down. I am a bit stiff.

It's odd; though he sits on his rear end for thousands of miles, I never see Jack Kerouac's Sal Paradise complaining about being stiff in *On the Road,* or Tom Wolfe mentioning an aching back in *The Electric Kool-Aid Acid Test,* or Elizabeth Bennet griping about her leg going to sleep as she and the Gardiners tour Derbyshire and enter the grounds of Pemberley in the greatest road trip book of all time, Jane Austen's *Pride and Prejudice,* but me? Road trips make me stiff as a pogo stick.

I put my bag down, as I say, and, sticking my left leg out behind me and slowly bending my right knee, I lower my ligaments, tendons, cartilage, bones, sprains, and strains down, down, down, down, dowwwwwwwwwwwn, till I am lying beside Miss Bingley and can look up her skirt and into her engine. Lewis Carroll, the poodle, clacking his teeth with a frantic expression, leans his blue flattop so far out Miss Bingley's back window, he could, with little effort, lie down beside me. Meanwhile, the wind is blowing my Donna Karan kilt up around my shoulders.

Ladies, we have all been to the gynecologist. It is not amusing. I reach my fingers up inside Miss Bingley, and with all possible tenderness, I touch her. She is very, *very* wet. Then I dabble my fingers in her damp puddle and smell my fingers.

Ha! HOOSIER MEN, *get out.*

"No worries, gentlemen," I say, rolling over and looking up at them sideways from under my cap.

"What is it? The radiator coolant?" says a chap with two mohawks, one over each ear.

"Naw," I say.

It's condensation from Miss Bingley's air-conditioning system. In other words: H$_2$O. But I don't tell them that. Instead, I ask:

"What do I need men for?"

"Huh?" says Mohawk.

"Can't you see she's ovulating?" I say.

As I hobble into the Brown County IGA, a thin young man of twenty-one or twenty-two, with large blue disks in his ears, Jared Leto hair, Indian beads, temple bells, and Whole Earth Catalog bell-bottoms is pushing a cart out the door and saying to the stout young woman in a huge tangerine sweatshirt, tight jeans, and tennis shoes walking behind him:

"I'm nothing but your punching bag and slave!"

"Whoa!" I cry.

I throw up a hand.

"I *can't* be in Indiana. I thought men ruled here."

"No," says the girl.

She shoots me an elevated look.

"*We* run things here."

This puts me in such a buoyant mood I fill my Brown County IGA cart to the brim with Amy's! Amy's! Amy's! Amy's! Amy's!

As a bonus to what has already been revealed about your advice columnist's mental endowments, Ladies, you should also know that you are reading a book written by a person who was the most boy-crazy seventeen-year-old in the nation.

If you had met me my freshman year at Indiana University in Bloomington, Indiana, right down the road from Gnaw Bone and seventy miles from Elnora, Indiana, you would never have imagined I was born to be your adviser, engine mechanic, and driver of Miss Bingley.

But imagine it now. Deep in the woods, three or four miles south of the IGA, there I am: seventeen-year-old Jeanie Carroll, driving with a boy down a hilly back road in Brown County State Park where IU students go on October Sundays to supposedly look at the famous leaves.

My situation in life, my father being a Beta Theta Pi from Wabash College, my mother being a Kappa Delta from UCLA, my wild wish to pledge either Pi Beta Phi or Kappa Kappa Gamma, my rah-rah disposition, my optimism, my total ignorance of what is going on in the world, the fact that I never crack a book and the university is compelled *by state law* to permit me to enroll as a freshman—all are equally against my becoming an advice columnist, the first requirement of which is acknowledging that there are other beings on the planet besides boys.

How I end up in that car, who the boy is—well . . . I don't remember his name. I've been looking through my 1961 datebook* and each day is so chock-full of the names of boys who called me, the names of boys who I expected to call me and didn't, the names of boys who did call me but I didn't care if they called me, the names of boys who if they didn't call me I was never going to speak to again, the names of boys who if they called me I would not pick up the phone, the names of boys who called me and left messages saying they were other boys calling me, and the names of boys I would have my roommate, Connie Kolker, call and ask if they called me while she was on the line with a boy who was begging me to call him back, I can't figure out who this boy is; but, Ladies, meet **#1 on The Most Hideous Men of My Life List.**

He belongs to that class of boys who are not athletes and so must make their mark on campus with their devastating looks or gobs of money. I don't remember this boy having either. I remember this boy's thing is his car. It is a stick shift. Nobody knows how to "drive a stick," he says, except him and A. J. Foyt, the Indianapolis 500 winner, and so I am amazed when he releases the clutch like he's stepping on a yellow-jacket nest and grinds the gears when he pulls over in the dirt and stops.

I look around. "I gotta get back to the dorm," I say.

He turns off the engine.

"Youuuuuuuu liiiittttttttttllllllllllll prrrrrrrrrrrrik teeeeeeeeeeez," he says. This opening compliment, "You little prick tease," is paid to every girl at some point or other in 1961, and I don't wait to be paid another. I open the car door and slide out.

What am I wearing? Tennis shoes, jeans, big sweatshirt, and—BLAM, he lunges from the car and bolts his arms around me. We crash, like felled trees, to the ground.

We land in grass covered in yellow leaves. Thanks to Mr. Weber, my high school biology teacher who promised Roger

---

* It is actually a 1962 datebook—I bought it when I arrived at school and all they had were the new 1962s.

McNett (Camera Club president, Service Club, Hi-Y sergeant-at-arms, Junior Academy of Science, Industrial Arts Recognition) and me (Best Athlete) each an A if we could find prothallium, the sexual form of a fern, inciting Roger and me to crawl on our hands and knees under almost every bridge and around every woody bog between Huntertown and Churubusco, Indiana, looking for prothallium and learning to identify trees *accidentally* in our way—the only remotely intellectual pursuit besides reading Dear Abby and looking for arrowheads with Dad I'd ever experienced in my life—I can, with 100 percent confidence, say those yellow leaves are poplar leaves.

They crackle as I struggle to get up. Straddling me, proud that he's battled a girl to the ground, the boy looks zonked out of his mind with the possibilities. He pushes my sweatshirt up to my neck.

I remember the thought flashes through my mind that could I have foreseen the circumstance of a boy throwing me down and pushing my sweatshirt up to my chin, I would not have worn a padded bra.

"I don't want to wrestle," I say. "Get off!"

Another time—another time! My God! I am telling you about a boy knocking me to the ground and I'm suddenly remembering *another* boy knocking me to the ground—a boy I have not remembered for sixty-two years, so now I guess he is **#2** on **The Most Hideous Men of My Life List.** He was a big, bony kid with immense shoulders and brindle hair that hung over his face, and he menaced me for weeks the summer I was thirteen.

He caught me alone one afternoon when I was practicing "walking the dog" with my yo-yo and threw me down on the lawn in Mary Jane Miller's backyard. Mary Jane was my friend and lived around the corner on Beaver Avenue in Fort Wayne in a pretty two-story house with a garden that had so many flowers there was almost no yard at all, but the kid had found a patch of grass big enough for him to climb on top of me and begin to try to yank down my shorts. He was yanking the shorts when Mary Jane came around the side of her house, and, screaming, she started kicking the kid, and Mary Jane's mother came running out the back door shrieking, "RICHARD! RICHARD! RICHARD! " It required both mother and daughter to drag him off. I believe Mary Jane's mother called his parents. Whoever she called he never appeared on the whole south side of Fort Wayne after that.

This boy, this IU boy, is pinning my arms over my head and hurting my wrists.

"Get off!" I say, again.

He is holding my wrists with both his hands, and, before I can react, he changes his hold to one hand, and, with his free hand, pulls a knife out of his back pocket.

"See this?" he whispers.

I look at it. At the time, I own two Girl Scout knives, a Girl Scout Knife Safety Certificate, my own personal hatchet, and the neighbor kids believe I have reached a height of felicity rarely attained on Illsley Place, our street, because of my winning about thirty rounds of mumbly-peg, a game where we throw pocketknives at each other's bare feet. So, yes, I can "see" his knife. It's a jackknife, a knife with a folding blade, dark brownish gray, made out of some kind of horn about five or six inches. If he opens it, it will measure, end-to-end, ten or eleven inches. It's not the knife. Well, it *is* the knife, but it's the look on his face that scares me.

"Get off," I say.

He pushes my padded bra up, over my breasts. I can smell his excitement; it's like electrified butter, and I zero in on the fact that he must use two hands to open the knife.

"Get off!" I say.

"I *am* gonna get off,'" he whispers.

He lets go of both of my wrists for two seconds to open the knife, and I roll out from under him and *run*.

I am not a fast runner. Though when I was fourteen and a half, the local papers covered my unstupendous athletic career as if I were Wilma Rudolph. The Fort Wayne *Journal Gazette* (or the *News-Sentinel*—I can't tell from the clipping which) later wrote:

> Jeanie Carroll set grade school speed-skating records, and established water skiing records at Lake Geneva, Wisconsin.
>
> As a 5'9", 110 pound high school freshman . . . she participated in the 1958 Nationals [in the high jump event] in Chicago and was even tendered an invitation to compete in the 1958 United States–Russian track meet in Russia.*

Dad and I *did* drive to Chicago for *a* track meet. This was before the Title IX era when there were no track events in Fort Wayne for females. Dad and I arrived at the stadium in Chicago early, and, as the high jumping was not scheduled till midafternoon, on a whim, Dad entered me in a qualifying heat of the hundred-yard dash "just to see what you can do."

In my neat white shorts and white sleeveless jersey with its jaunty red stripe across the chest emblazoned with the glamorous words FORT WAYNE, I looked like a winner. And then, unfortunately, the starter fired her pistol.

"Jeanie was so slow," my dad used to say when he told the story, "if she hadn't picked up her feet at the end, she'd have finished in the middle of the next heat."

No matter—I outrun this boy. I pull down my sweatshirt and I run like—my God! I've just remembered when I was fifteen, there was a tall cadet at the Culver Military Academy who tried to throw me on the ground—my God! I don't believe it. Lord!

---

* Naw-naw-naw-naw. Let's fact-check this thing. I did not "set records" in speed-skating or water-skiing. The "Nationals" were in Cleveland, not Chicago. I may have qualified (perhaps by merely showing up) to receive an invitation to Russia, but the US Track and Field team would not have paid for it.

This is nuts. I'm sorry about this pileup, Ladies, but here is a jolting **#3** on **The Most Hideous Men of My Life List**. The cadet maneuvered me behind one of the buildings and tried to jam his hand up my skirt, and when I took off running, he pursued me across the Culver campus in the dark with his fellow mercenaries cheering him on like it was the Charge of the Light Brigade. My GOD! This is—Ladies, I beg your pardon. I have to go eat a bowl of oatmeal.

4 ·········▶

Pondering the fact that you probably weren't even born when I was running across the Culver campus—*hell,* what am I saying? Your *parents* probably weren't born—and thinking about how many years I have the start on you—calculating how many more years I have lived among men on this planet, and how many more years men have had the "opportunity" to chase me, prick me, bruise me, maul me, prod me, thump me, I have come to the conclusion that I should no longer be rattled that I recall three instances of being thrown to the ground. The wonder is that I don't recall *more.*

But to go on: I was fifteen when I was at Culver with my friend Linda Crowe, visiting her brother. I must have run to her parents' friends' house—I can't remember, I think the husband was the chief academic officer or something, because the boys stopped cheering when I reached a hundred yards of the front door.

And Brown County State Park and the IU boy with the stick shift? On a twisty back road through tangled orange-and-scarlet thickets, a young couple in a car picked me up about a quarter hour after I escaped, and the girl said, "I'll bet a boy tried something with you," and I said, "Yeah," and that was the last word I uttered about the attack until this minute.

Had I been an artist, I could have carried the front seat of the car the boy was driving wherever I went on Indiana University's campus to protest his assault like Emma Sulkowicz carrying her mattress around Columbia University in the greatest art show of 2014, but I didn't think of it. Perhaps hauling around just the gearshift would have sufficed. But, like many women who are attacked, when I had the most to say, I said the least.

Let's just double-check my diary:

Do I write that I went to the campus police and reported the boy? Do I say I went to the university health clinic and talked with a therapist? No. Next to Saturday, October 6, when I announce that I "started smoking," that I cheered as an Indiana University pom-pom girl at my first Big Ten football game, and that I plan to devastate a Phi Gam named Pete Cajacobs, on the Monday, October 8 page (I had taken up the diary space provided for Sunday, October 7—the actual day of the Brown County date—writing about other boys named Larry and Pico calling), I say:

BE IT KNOWN—
That from this day forth I will not except [sic] or go on any dates that are not of my choice—they must be boys who are to my liking [I can't read what I crossed out here]. I have to [sic] many things to do—rather than waste my time with CREEPY BOYS.
   (signed)
Jeanie Carroll

The Freshman

Miss Bingley rockets along, the purple and gold treetops streaming across her windshield, her speakers wailing *Death on the Nile* by Agatha Christie, Lewis Carroll grinning and breaking wind in her back seat. It's a beautiful What Do We Need Men For day, Ladies!

We peel at last into rickety, proud Elnora, and, looking about, we skim up Ellen Street, can't find Adaline Street, turn around, lose our bearings—and Miss Bingley's bearings are always a concern—on Ida Street, find ourselves again on Matilda Street, turn around and, as I have promised Lewis Carroll a treat, I slide Miss Bingley under the blue-and-pink portico of the Circle K gas station and convenience store and scoot inside.

Ladies! You have never beheld such marvels inside a gas station toilet in your lives! We have a choice:

For only three quarters, we can possess **A)** The Tingler, a glow-in-the-dark doodlebanger ring with tiny thorns jutting out all around it. From the picture, it looks like a cross between a spiked collar for a pit bull and Billy Idol's hair from 1985. The Tingler promises to "prolong the pleasure of sex" and "achieve total sexual fulfillment together."

B) The Love Kit. I don't know what is *in* the Love Kit, but as it says it will bring "romance and fun," I suppose it could be a tiny rich man who likes forty-five minutes of foreplay.

Or **C)** The Hugger—not a pill to make a bloke cuddle after sex, as I first hope. No. It is a "premium latex condom" which is "made slimmer for a tighter fit" and is "electronically tested to meet FDA standards."

I run out of the bathroom shouting to the clerk behind the counter, "Quarters! Quarters! Quarters!"

She looks at me, alarmed.

"I've just been visiting your toilet, Miss—?"

"Anita," she says.

"And *what* is in your toilet, Miss Anita?"

Miss Anita, standing tall in her ring of cash and gas pump registers, proves to be an outstanding light-heavyweight, wearing a crimson pullover, with a magnificent bosom and a spectacular cackling laugh that sounds like *Ack Ack Ack Ack Ack Ack Ack Ack.* She has a big chin, fluffy Farrah Fawcett bangs, long, wavy brown hair down to her shoulders, and braids, one on each side of her head, swinging exhilaratingly back and forth as she bursts into joyful *Ack Ack Ack Ack Ack*s.

"You tell *me!*" she says, pushing up her tortoiseshell glasses with her index finger. "I don't look at 'em. I try to *avoid* them."

"Should I get The Tingler, and we can see what it's all about?"

"*Ack Ack Ack Ack Ack Ack Ack Ack Ack Ack Ack Ack Ack Ack Ack Ack Ack Ack Ack Ack Ack Ack Ack Ack!* Noooooooo!" says Miss Anita, gripping the counter, rocking back and forth, cackling and pushing up her glasses.

"Hang on!" I run into the bathroom, which is about ten steps from Miss Anita's counter. "OK!" I shout out the door. "Which do you want? THE TINGLER? THE LOVE KIT, OR THE HUGGER?"

"*Ack Ack Ack Ack Ack Ack Ack Ack Ack Ack Ack Ack Ack Ack Ack Ack Ack Ack Ack Ack Ack Ack Ack Ack Ack Ack Ack Ack Ack Ack Ack Ack Ack Ack Ack Ack Ack Ack Ack.*"

I come out. I forget I don't have any quarters.

"Is this pretty much what goes on all the time here in fabulous Elnora, Indiana?" I say.

"Haumuph!" Miss Anita with a cackle-snort.

Every single one of her front teeth go in a different direction.

"So, if we can get the spectacular Love Kit for seventy-five cents, What Do We Need Men For?"

The question nearly kills Miss Anita and starts her *Ack Ack Ack Ack Ack*ing, and her braids slap back and forth with such force I'm afraid one will put out an eye.

"We need 'em for a *lot* of things!" she says.

"Well . . . what for?" I say.

Miss Anita stops cackling, tilts her head to the side, and looks at me over her cash register with a wise smile.

"All kinds of things," she says.

"Well . . . name three."

"Job security! Children! Moral support!" Boom. Boom. Boom.

"But do you really *neeeeeeed*—"

She cuts me off.

"Yup!"

"You *really* need—"

"YUP!!!"

"Don't you think the world would be a better place if it were run by women?"

Miss Anita slams her lips together and lifts her chin.

"Nope."

"Well, why can't women run the world better?"

As we talk, I see through the window old Lewis Carroll leaning out Miss Bingley waiting for his treat and Hoosiers filling up with gas. The chaps are skinny, built on the all-bone-and-balls design. The women are lusty, constructed on the exploding airbag design. And so I wonder how they make love to each other without the blokes' bony elbows poking out the eardrums of the females, and without the females crushing the gaunt males under their billowy curvature, and I make a mental note to double-check the population of Elnora.*

---

* According to the 2010 census, it is 640, down 81 souls from 2000.

"Why can't women run the world?" I repeat. "Is it because of Adam and Eve?" This is not a wild guess. Lewis and I passed the Elnora Bible Institute on the way into town.

"Eve got what she deserved!" says Anita, pushing up her glasses. "It was her *own* fault!"

"*Please*," I say. "Now don't tell me that *you*, the brilliant Anita, wouldn't have eaten that fruit? *Come on . . .* really, come *on*."

"Nope."

"You wouldn't have—?"

[Vehemently.] "NOPE!"

"Wait. *You* are telling *me* that you wouldn't be tempted to attain ALL THE KNOWLEDGE IN THE WORLD, which is

what the snake promised, if you simply ate a dinky piece of *fruit?*"

"Nope!"

I peer at her, smiling, trying to figure out her thinking. "So then," I say, "Eve ate the fruit, and the Lord punished—"

"That's *right!*"

She pushes up her glasses in a "Finally, we're down to business" manner using *two* fingers.

I have eight parts of speech, but it is rare that I quote the Bible.

"'And the Lord sayeth to Eve,'" I repeat slowly, "'He shall rule over thee.'"

"That's *riiiiight!*" says Miss Anita softly, the brightest glow overspreading her face and her braids lying exhausted on her shoulders. "Men's gonna rule over women. That's the way it's *supposed* to be."

At this interesting point, Miss Anita's boss comes by and tells me to stop videoing Miss Anita and for Miss Anita to "get back to work." I buy a banana Popsicle for Lewis, and, bidding fond adieu to Miss Anita, *vamoose.*

So, let's tote up the score, Ladies.

Number of reasons we need men? **3***

Number of reasons we don't need men? **9,000,000,000†**

Pretty good start to our trip, wouldn't you say?

---

* *Per* Anita: 1. Job security. 2. Children. 3. Moral support.

† I am not a Bible scholar like Anita. My Bible is the Old and New Testament of the Almighty Jane Austen. But even *I,* half-wit that I am, know there are *two* creation stories in Genesis—chapter 1 and chapter 2, and chapter 1 doesn't even *mention* Adam and Eve. It simply states: "So God created man in his own image, in the image of God created him; male and female created he them."

Only later, in chapter 2 of Genesis, do we get the old Sumerian tales with characters named Adam and Eve, a garden called Eden, a snake, a temptation, and a peeved cracker called the "LORD" in all caps declaring "He shall rule over thee" and other general schmuckery.

So, Ladies, here's what I figure:

The number of Jewish, Catholic, Lutheran, Mormon, Baptist, Methodist, Presbyterian, Congregationalist, Seventh-Day Adventist, Evangelical Christian, and Anglican priests, ministers, bishops, deacons, chaplains, rectors, elders, preachers, patriarchs, abbots, lectors, cantors, beadles, cardinals, and rabbis who have been selling the men-should-rule-over-women-chapter-2-hogwash to control women over the last 2,400 years amounts to—my estimation is necessarily cursory here—9 billion.

II

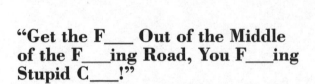

"Get the F___ Out of the Middle of the F___ing Road, You F___ing Stupid C___!"

Cynthiana, Indiana
(#15,441 Most Popular Girl's Name)

Once upon a time, billboards—massive things, stupefying, thrilling, incredible, unbelievable, 14 feet high, 48 feet wide, 672 square feet—sprang up like monoliths here, and by *here,* I mean all over the state of Indiana. They featured your traveling companion and advice columnist. Yup.

The whole state was slathered with giant images of an ecstatic Jeanie escaped from her bottle, soaring above the stunned crowd in the Indiana University football stadium, a big *I* on my sweater, skirt aswirl, legs split like the atom.

And, Ladies, I've never really come down . . . have I?

I'm up there, perpetually, eternally, forever in mid-leap, urging the crowd to never lose hope. I was a cheerleader in grade school. I was a cheerleader in high school. My sisters, Cande and Barbie, were cheerleaders; my brother, Tom, was a pole-vaulter, so he jumped too. Today, I open an Ask E. Jean letter, I read the question, and what do I do, Ladies? I start shouting and yelling and cheering at the correspondent to pick herself up and go on. And, by God! The correspondent *does* pick herself up and *does* go on! Because if she doesn't, I keep yelling at her.

I am on the billboards because the Indiana University Athletic Department nominates me to represent our great institution in the Miss Cheerleader USA contest in Cypress Gardens, Florida. I make the Final Five, and, wearing a flamingo-pink polyester dress, white gloves, and a pink pillbox hat, I fly to Florida.

On the afternoon of the contest, following forty-eight hours of
press dinners, water-skiing, modeling Catalina swimsuits, fend-
ing off Chamber of Commerce libertines, and photo-ops with
the other finalists—extremely talented young lady-cheerleaders
hailing from Austin Peay State University, Auburn University,
Birmingham Southern College, and Ohio University, all sweat-
ing like yaks in their hot cheerleading sweaters and wool skirts—I
leap onto the outdoor stage with its enormous backdrop of a
football made of flowers.

The crowd is fanatical. I receive a sitting ovation.

The other finalists are great, fantastic, brilliant; they have performed with extraordinary pep and zeal. Miss Auburn's cheer is "Beat Bama." Miss Ohio's cheer is something about how Ohio will lay waste and tear everyone to bloody shreds who dares come near them. Miss Austin Peay's cheer is about "rimming" and "ramming," and Miss Birmingham Southern's accent is so melodious, I'm not certain what her cheer is about, but I clap my hands and yell for her, and when my turn comes, I raise my voice and start in exuberantly leading the crowd in spelling out INDIANA.

I am not wearing my official Indiana University cheerleading uniform, which is ugly, with the pleated skirt to my knees, Ladies, *to my knees*. No. No. No. No. No. I have *made* my outfit. I have designed it specifically for the hellish heat of Florida: a short, pleated, narrow, crimson jumper with a white *I* on the bosom, over a sleek white turtleneck—very Givenchy. Very Audrey Hepburn.

So there I am on stage with the giant football made of flowers in an outfit that could have appeared in the opening scene of *Breakfast at Tiffany's* spelling out I N-D-I-A-N-A, and I stop right in the middle of it and, maintaining a strict silence, turn my back on the crowd.

I feel them staring up at me, squirming with a nameless dread.

One of the Miss Cheerleader USA officials standing backstage raises her eyes to the heavens and rapidly fans herself with the program. George Bush, Reese Witherspoon, Jimmy Stewart, Meryl Streep, Diane Sawyer, Dwight D. Eisenhower, Katie Couric, Amy Poehler, Madonna, Sandra Bullock, Halle Berry, and Ruth Bader Ginsburg were all cheerleaders. Cheerleaders never give up. I turn. I face the crowd, frown, clutch my head, and shout:

"Oh! My! That was terrible!"

They have bused in high school cheerleaders from all over

Florida, and their stout cheerleader hearts are nearly breaking with pity for me. The judges are looking at one another in a semi-panic. Am I not the contestant who had done so well in the water-skiing? Had I not whizzed along behind that speedboat, jumping back and forth over the wake like a great white pelican on Adderall? Had not my fancy pageant strut drowned the competition at the Catalina swimsuit photo shoots? This, of course, is before ESPN2 started running all the cheerleading contests—actually, this is fifteen *years* before ESPN.

"Darn it all!" I shout to the crowd. "Are you from Indiana?"

The cheerleaders in the crowd perk up.

"NO!" they shout.

"Does anybody even know how to *spell* Indiana?"

"NO!" they scream happily.

"Well . . . . . . Is anybody here from Florida?"

"YESSSSSSS!!!!!!"

GIVE ME AN F!

efffff!

GIVE ME AN L!

eLLLLLLLL!

GIVE ME AN O!

OOOOOooooooo!

GIVE ME AN R!

Rrrrrrrr!

GIVE ME AN I!

Iiiiiiiii!

GIVE ME A D!

Deeeeeee!

GIVE ME AN A!

Aaaaaaaa!

WHAT HAVE YOU GOT??

I.U.'s Jeannie Carroll . . . Miss Cheerleader U.S.A.   Story inside

3

My photo (in a swimsuit!) plays on front pages across the nation. A month later, I fly to New York and appear on the television show *To Tell the Truth*. I meet President Johnson in the Rose Garden. I get a big scholarship. I have done the thing no Indiana University football team has *ever* done—I have won a national championship, and its importance to the Indiana Athletic Department is pretty great.

I am as happy a being as ever existed. And following a very short bus ride, I am looking forward to an even grander event than Miss Cheerleader:

Forty thousand boys awaiting me and my rhinestone crown. It is Spring Break at Daytona Beach, and, Ladies, 1964 is the year we *invent* Spring Break.

Unfortunately, about six hours after my sorority sisters hear the big news on the radio and run shrieking and leaping across the beach to greet me as I arrive at our Daytona motel, the bottom of my face explodes in cold sores—a reaction to my last two days in the Cypress Gardens sun. From nostrils to chin, I look like a farmer has dragged a harrow across my face and turned up bright red clods. Except for one moonlight walk on the beach with Sven Groennings, I spend the next four days *inside*.

4 ·············▶

Sven is a very fashionable-looking, tall, handsome, young Indiana University professor of political science (and glamorous winner of the Graham Stuart Award as Stanford University's most outstanding political science graduate) with cheekbones like Ping-Pong paddles and a Norwegian? Swedish? Finnish? accent. When we all return to school and classes begin, I don greaser shades and a trench coat, and, with nothing on underneath except my yellow bikini, I crash one of Sven's lectures in the big Ballantine lecture auditorium, walk across the front of the stage, flash him repeatedly, and subject the man to a nervous strain unparalleled in the halls of academe until the moment twenty years later when Harold Bloom, the celebrated Yale humanities professor, allegedly places his hand on the illustrious inner thigh of Naomi Wolf (he denies it), she throws up in the sink and we all talk about it in books and magazines for the next two decades.

I tell this little story to explain #4 on **The Most Hideous Men of My Life List.** Today, if a man walked into a classroom and flashed a female professor, that man would hopefully be jailed. So, Ladies, it should come as no surprise that #4 on **The Most Hideous Men of My Life List** is me.

My mother once saw a black bear looking over the windowsill of my cabin in the Wawayanda Mountains of New York. On her deathbed, sixteen years later, thinking of her cat, Ma's last words—her last words!—to me were:

"Don't take Kitty Carroll home with you."

"Don't take Kitty Carroll."

"I *won't* take Kitty Carroll, Ma."

"Promise me, Jeanie."

"I promise, Ma!"

"Don't take Kitty Carroll."

"I promise! I won't take Kitty Carroll!"

"The bears . . ."

"Don't worry, Ma!"

[Silence.]

"Don't take . . ."

"I won't!"

"Don't . . ."

"I won't!"

[Long silence.]

"Don't . . ."

"I won't!"

Shortly after this conversation, when 100 percent finally assured by my sister Barbie that Yvonne Vanderbilt, my mother's friend, was taking Kitty Carroll, only *then,* after ninety-eight fabulous years on the planet, wearing Volcanic #410 lipstick, Oscar de la Renta hostess pajamas, and her hair done up in a turquoise bow, did Ma shuffle off this mortal coil.

Six weeks later, Kitty Carroll bid yowling adieu to Yvonne Vanderbilt and her elegant house following a disagreement about where Kitty Carroll's toilet was: Yvonne thought it was the litter box; Kitty Carroll thought it was Yvonne's bed.

This is how I ended up with Ma's cat.

So that wherever she is in the cosmos, Ma won't find out I broke my promise, I changed Kitty Carroll's name to Vagina T. Fireball, and at this moment, I am sitting at an intersection in tired but verdant Cynthiana, Indiana, with its white houses and vegetable gardens, reading Vagina T. Fireball *updates* that my twelve-year-old neighbor, Bella, to whom I'm paying fifteen dollars a day for cat duty, texts me. Here is the last picture I took (outside . . . *in the dark*) before I left:

If Ma weren't already dead, this photo would kill her. I considered bringing Vagina T. along on the What Do We Need Men For trip. Why not? Nellie Bly, in her famous 1889 race to beat the record set by Phileas Fogg in Jules Verne's *Around the World in Eighty Days,* circled half the globe accompanied by a monkey.

I have Lewis Carroll, of course, and four Global Huntress cinder-gray nylon bags measuring 27.2 × 13.9 inches each, in which I have packed:

IN BAG A

- 1 Vivienne Westwood brown tweed jacket
- 1 Vivienne Westwood marengo-gray "artist smock" raincoat with sash
- 1 Ariat equestrian vest

1 Wedgwood-blue fuzzy wool hat with pom-pom (we are traveling in October and November), hand knit by a woman named Katherine who resides in Russia

1 white-tan-rose-turquoise scarf knit by my sister Cande

1 Black Watch tartan scarf from Scotland

6 cowgirl bandannas, assorted colors

1 Mac Air computer sandwiched between the coats

IN BAG B

8 sets of Uniqlo long underwear in black (worn as T-shirts and leggings), also worn as pajamas

5 kilts (1 Donna Karan and 4 "authentic" tartans from Scotland)

6 pairs of Ann Taylor tights

1 Lisa Birnbach cast-off navy-blue turtleneck

1 Lisa Birnbach cast-off aubergine velvet Highland jacket

3 Gwyneth Paltrow Goop sleep bras (to wear when not sleeping)

36 No-Nonsense white cuff socks*

IN BAG C

2 jars of Vaseline

1 jar of Aquaphor

1 jar of Garnier SkinActive Moisture Rescue Refreshing Gel-Cream

1 tube of L'Oréal EverPure Sulfate-Free Blonde Brass Banisher Shampoo

1 tube of L'Oréal EverPure Sulfate-Free Blonde Brass Banisher Conditioner

1 tube of Crest 3D White Fluoride Anticavity toothpaste

---

* When traveling, I never wash socks. I buy them, wear them, leave them in the room. (And I do not walk across motel room carpets in my bare feet. See footnote on page 74 *Immediately!*)

1 Colgate toothbrush (soft)

1 comb

bobby pins

1 mirror

1 eyebrow plucker

1 bottle of Bayer aspirin

1 bottle of Advil

1 bottle of Tylenol*

1 sewing kit

1 box of Kleenex

1 small ziplock sandwich bag with:

    Sephora retractable, waterproof eyeliner in black

    1 tube of Revlon's Toast of New York lipstick

    1 tube of Garnier 5-in-1 Miracle Skin Protector in light/
       medium with Broad Spectrum SPF 15

2 blunt-cut wigs, both red.

IN BAG D

4 blank 7 × 5-inch Caliber spiral notebooks in red, green,
    yellow, blue

20 Pilot G2 #07 ballpoint pens in navy blue, black, bur-
    gundy, violet, caramel, hunter green, pink, turquoise,
    orange, periwinkle, lime, and red

1 Rand McNally Road Atlas with "35% larger maps"

3 miniature LUX-PRO Trendz flashlights

cords

batteries

extra cords

---

* And don't tell old E. Jean that Zelda Fitzgerald didn't pack a ton of aspirin when she
and Scott made their epic road trip from Connecticut to Alabama ("for biscuits and
peaches"), which Scott writes about in *The Cruise of the Rolling Junk*, on roads—mostly
unpaved—that had to be bumpy as *hell* in 1920!

extra batteries
extra flashlights
extra pens
extra notebooks
1 ziplock bag with:
.   wine opener, can opener, knife, fork, and spoon
1 bowl
1 roll of Bounty paper towels
1 loaf of organic whole wheat bread
1 jar of organic crunchy peanut butter
1 jar of organic strawberry jam

In Miss Bingley's roomy underdeck storage, we have six bottles of wine with women's names on the labels (e.g., Mommy's Time Out, a Pinot Grigio, etc.); seventy cans of Amy's Organic Chili, Amy's Organic Spicy Chili, Amy's Organic Black Bean Chili, Amy's Organic Chili with Vegetables, Amy's Organic Vegetarian Baked Beans, Amy's Organic Refried Black Beans, Eden Organic Black Beans, Eden Organic Pinto Beans, Eden Organic Garbanzo Beans, Eden Organic Black-Eyed Peas, Eden Organic Black Soybeans, Eden Organic Lentils with Onion and Bay, Eden Organic Chili Beans; plus fifty or sixty packages of Purely Elizabeth Ancient Grain Oatmeal, plus the Girl Scout cookies, though we are stopping at Dairy Queen and cafés named after women daily, if not hourly.

And Nellie Bly? What did that magnificent journalist pack for her around-the-earth trip in 1889? What did she carry when every American citizen from sea to shining sea was cheering as she traveled the last leg of her trip from San Francisco to New York at incredible speeds of nearly fifty miles per hour on a special train ordered by Joseph Pulitzer? How many bags and trunks did she have when the ten-gun salute was fired from Battery Park as she stepped off the train in Jersey City and for the first time in the history of the world, a woman circumnavigated the globe "without guide, escort or attendant?"*

Trunks? None. Suitcases? Zero. Miss Bly wore one skirt, one bodice, one hat, and one coat for the entire seventy-two-day journey! She carried one small handbag—about the size of a Birkin—with toiletries, changes of underwear, paper and pens, and, Ladies, she arrived, with the monkey, looking *smashing*.

I won't mention what I have packed here beside me in Miss Bingley's front seat (just the Scout bag with an *Elle* magazine, my wallet, my phone, my current notebook, three pens, one Sharpie, plus a box on the floor with Lewis's portable drinking bowl, more paper towels, more Vaseline, more cords, eight grapefruits, etc.), but I will mention that of all the fellow travelers I've observed on this trip, the lightest traveler, lighter even than Jack Reacher, the person traveling with the least amount of crap is the only person I meet who is 100 percent stumped by the question, "What Do We Need Men For?"

Her chestnut hair is cut in a Jean Seberg, and I chase her down the middle of the street of Cynthiana, Indiana.

She wears red corduroys—so very, *very* chic—and black-framed spectacles and is at the controls of a high-tech wheelchair, the whole forming a dashing tout ensemble.

"Hi!" I yell, stomping the brakes of Miss Bingley, hurling Lewis Carroll to the floor, and jumping out in front of the girl. "I

---

* *The New York World*, January 25, 1890.

am going to towns named after women and asking people: What Do We Need Men For?"

She looks up at me, flabbergasted. She holds my eyes so long that I laugh and repeat the question.

"What Do We Need Men For?"

She glances at Lewis Carroll, who, once again on his seat, is leaning out his window, clacking his teeth and lashing up a grin on an impressive scale. She smiles, looks back at me, and lifts her hands in pained confusion.

"Ma'am?" she says.

"What do we need the chaps, the lads, the boys, the men for? I'm driving across the country and asking because I have an excellent plan for getting *rid* of men. But first I have to figure out if we *need* them for anything."

This puts the young woman under such a torment of anxiety to do her best to help and assist me that the thought crosses my mind we should both just biff down the road to Fort Branch and inhale a couple of martinis at Fat Boys Tavern.

"What do we *need* 'em for?" I say encouragingly.

Intellectual turmoil shines from her every feature.

"I can't say, ma'am."

I spin in such exultation, I nearly fall over.

"*We-e-e-e-e-lllll!*" I cry. "*Of course* you can't say. It's *impossible!*" And I am about to add, "It's useless because we don't need men for *anything . . .*" when I am cut off mid-sentence by the entrance, at the end of the block, of a beautiful, shiny pickup truck, so bright and glossy I can almost see my reflection in it when it pulls up and the man behind the wheel BLAAAAARR-RRRRS his horn.

"Get the fuck out of the middle of the fucking road, you fucking stupid cunt!" he shouts at me, along with some other sonnets to my wit and beauty, which I can't hear because his windows are up *and* he starts honking again.

Now, all the fellow has to do is turn his steering wheel *four inches* to the left and go around us. But no.

I turn to the girl.

"Bah!" I say. "Men are so emotional."

III

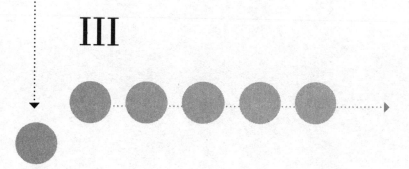

"I'd Kill Him!"

Anita, Indiana
(#1,147 Most Popular Girl's Name)

"I'm getting a divorce."

"Good for you!" says the sandy-haired motel clerk.

"I'll give him whatever he wants."

"Good riddance!" says the motel clerk, taking the woman's credit card.

"I want *out!*" says the woman.

I look around.

Out? I'm standing in line behind the woman, a few miles outside Anita, Indiana, and poor little Anita is so "out" that Google Maps classifies it as "extinct."

"We have a court date," says the woman, "in Indianapolis."

The desk clerk, who has been typing something into the Hardwick Inn and Suites computer, takes hold of the stapler.

"You'll sue that jerk!" she says, and whacks the stapler on the counter.

"No," says the woman. "Whatever he wants, I'm giving it to him."

A fellow woman announcing she wants to "give" a man "whatever he wants" is a circumstance to strike your advice columnist deeply, Ladies.

I have been idly standing behind the woman, assessing her ponytail, which is not simply a ponytail, but a *high* ponytail—the sign of female confidence!—and I can tell you, Ladies, without reserve, that in normal circumstances, I would be *riveted* to the ponytail, as I am a great ponytail aficionado and can rank the greatest ponytails I've seen in my life, First Place going to a dark-haired teenager in a white speedboat on Clear Lake, Indiana; Second Place going to a Kappa Kappa Gamma with hair so black it was blue, competing in cheerleading tryouts at UCLA, etc., etc., and, if circumstances were different, I'd be, at this very moment, ranking the Anita, Indiana, ponytail—which, in fact, reaches halfway to the woman's waist and is of that stupendous shade of fire-apple red one only sees growing from the heads of exceptional Hoosiers. But I'm becoming so caught up in the woman's conversation, I forgo the ponytail, step forward, and put my hand on the woman's arm.

"Pardon me," I say. "No doubt you are correct, but—"

The woman turns and looks at me.

Korean driving cap, Donna Karan maroon-and-black tartan kilt, Ann Taylor tights, three-tone saddle shoes with black gros-grain bows the size of hydrangeas, and, on a leash, a giant Cream-sicle-colored poodle with an electric-blue flattop who is wearing a seventeenth-century ruff of red, yellow, green, purple, pink, gold, and blue ribbons. (Ruff! Ruff!) Yet the woman with the ponytail looks right at me *and* the dog and does not flinch.

This woman knows weirdness.

"Stop and consider," I say to her. "Is it wise to give your husband *everything?*"

The woman glances from me to the very young motel clerk whose foot-long bangs are combed straight down and across her right eye.

"I already sold my house up in South Bend," says the woman, "with the five bedrooms when my ex-husband died in a car crash."

"Oh! Good Heavens!" I cry. "That's terrible. You lost your husband!"

"No. My *first* husband died," says the woman. "Then I moved me and the kids down here and used the money from the house I sold to buy a house for me and the husband I'm divorcing now."

"Ah!"

"And you know what he did?" says the woman.

"No," says the motel clerk.

"He put the house *I* bought in his parents' names."

"*What?!*" I cry.

"No way!" says the motel clerk.

"Yeah," says the woman. "I just found out. I caught him cheating on me for the third time and started looking into things."

"My ex-husband cheated on me for fifteen years!" says the motel clerk.

I stare at the motel clerk, petrified with delight.

Not because she was cheated on by her husband for fifteen years—a horrible, terrible torment. Anyone who's read a stack of Ask E. Jeans knows the score on *that* topic. It's the fact that the motel clerk barely appears old enough to *be* a motel clerk, let alone to have lived long enough on the planet to have been plagued for fifteen years by a cheating husband, and yet here she is looking as victorious as a college girl who just won the javelin throw in a track meet. And I can explain why I'd guessed her to be so young:

Unlike people in New York, Los Angeles, Houston, Atlanta, Seattle, San Francisco, Philadelphia, Chicago, etc., in most Indiana towns, people are not marketing themselves yet as personal brands, and many Hoosier women still favor a style of dress in which the rest of us would not be caught dead but which, considering the times we live in, we might do well to consider for the following reasons:

Firstly: The Hoosier Style covers the backs of the arms, the neck, the waist, and the tops of the thighs, giveaways for age.

Secondly: The Hoosier Style does not feature high heels, and one can run from one's attacker, stalker, harasser, drunk husband, randy boss, etc., while wearing it.

Thirdly: The Hoosier-Style top is roomy enough that a woman wearing it can move freely to defend herself and/or carry two kids on her shoulders and/or three babies in her arms when a man who's stockpiled seven automatic rifles modified with bump stocks starts mowing down shoppers at a mall.

The Hoosier Style, in short, consists of what people in Indiana call "tennis shoes," tight jeans, and an extra-super-large hooded sweatshirt—not the fitted Silicon Valley hoodie with the idiot tassels and the zip, no, but the big, *big* sweatshirt with the pouchy hand-warmer in front. It was what I was wearing when **#1 Most Hideous Man** attacked me in Brown County State Park. It was what the girl in the IGA parking lot was wearing when she said, *"We* run things here." The motel clerk's sweatshirt is dark emerald green, and she looks *awesome.*

Perfectly unsuspicious of the wonder that she is creating in the elderly advice columnist with the dog, the motel clerk continues: "He beat me and cheated on me the whole fifteen years."

"You know how I found out my husband was cheating on me?" says the woman with the ponytail.

I don't know which cheated-on woman to turn to first. Lewis Carroll, the poodle, who has a genius for raising pet fees charged by motels by the simple expedient of entering each new lobby at about thirty miles an hour, rearing up on his back legs, planting his front paws on the welcome desk, lunging at the clerk with a hello kiss, sniffing all crotches, and knocking down all children—even Lewis Carroll, I say, is sitting quietly at the redheaded woman's feet and looking up with an interested, but worried, expression from her to the motel clerk.

"How'd you find out he was cheating?" I say to the woman.

"I'm a hospice nurse," she says, "and he didn't have a job, but he always convinced me he needed the car to go on job interviews, so I walked to work almost every day."

"Walked!" I cry. I feel like Mrs. Elton chastising Jane Fairfax

for walking in the rain to the Highbury post office. "But a hospice nurse needs *all* her energy for her dying patients!"

The woman says quietly, "I know."

"You can't be walking to work, for God's sakes!" I say.

"I know! I know!" says the motel clerk, pushing aside her long bangs. "I just lost my father. The hospice nurses were wonderful!" Tears spring into her eyes, and without the least warning, a voice rings out.

"DON'T START CRYING, MOM!"

The lobby is timbered in the kind of wood that looks like it's been ripped out of an Austrian ski lodge, with big sofas in front of a massive TV and fireplace, and a glassed-in swimming pool—very UN-Hardwicky—Hardwick Inns are usually white and green with shrimplike outdoor pools. I had thought the lobby was empty, but a pretty teenager with long blond hair suddenly sits up and, turning about, looks at us severely from over the back of her sofa.

"I won't! I won't!" says the motel clerk, waving for her daughter to go back to reading her book.

"I walk to work practically every day," says the redheaded woman, "and then I find out he's driving over to his ex–baby mama's house and spending the whole day [lowering her voice] fucking her."

"No!" I cry.

"I'd kill him!" says the motel clerk. "I don't care if they send me to jail! It'd be worth it!"

"And every night he's coming home [air-quoting] *exhausted* from looking for work and tells *me* I look fat."

"*WHAT!?*" I scream.

The daughter sits up again and looks over.

"I had gained a little weight because of the regimen I was following after I survived stage 2 cancer," says the woman.

"My *God!*" I cry. "This is not even possible!"

"Oh, yes," says the woman. "It's possible. My daughter has lymphoma, and I had stage 2 cancer, and he was spending every day at his ex–baby mama's."

"But you have a lovely figure!" I say.

The redheaded woman steps back, slowly raises her arms from her sides, and modestly looks at me and the motel clerk. We gaze upon a figure in a magnificent extra-extra-large white hooded sweatshirt, tight-fitted jeans, and tennis shoes.

"*Please,*" I say.

I sweep an arm toward her like I am Ryan Seacrest on the red carpet greeting Emma Stone.

"He's full of shit," says the motel clerk.

"Wait," I say to the redheaded woman. "Pardon me. Didn't you mention something about your daughter?"

"She has lymphoma," says the woman.

"My God!" I cry. "May I go with you to court? Do you have friends to support you? Here, take my number, call me, text me whenever you need a—"

"I have wonderful friends!" says the redheaded woman, shutting me down and taking her room card from the motel clerk. "*Wonderful* friends!"

And so, with her stupendous ponytail swaying behind her reminding me of something or someone I can't quite place, she turns and heads toward the door.

"Heavens!" I say to the motel clerk. "That is too much for one woman."

The woman who "this is too much for" shouts back triumphantly as she goes out the door:

"*I'm a ginger! You can't stop me!*"

Men have had enough nice books written about them. Not this one, Ladies.

I hand the motel clerk my credit card and driver's license.

"My husband beat me and cheated on me for fifteen years," says the motel clerk, without an intermission. "He beat me over and over. I finally got smart, called the police, and left forever. He's in jail now."

"Good!" I say.

"Yeah, he also beat his current girlfriend almost to death. He's not getting out for a long time."

I, myself, have called the police. Or rather, my friend C. C. Dyer (*that's* who I'm reminded of—it's the red hair) thought about calling the police. She and her future husband, Geraldo Rivera, were visiting my husband and me. And now, Ladies, let me introduce **#5** on **The Most Hideous Men of My Life List:** the most splendid of all anchormen, the envy of the world, the delight of the universe—Mr. J. J. By the by, **The Most Hideous Men** on **The Most Hideous Men of My Life List** are not ranked in hideosity. I am simply putting them on the list as I remember them.

Geraldo and C. C. were visiting, as I say, and we were all at our house in the mountains outside Suffern—what a name!—New York. Early one morning, C. C. had sneaked down to our little knotty pine kitchen to make coffee, and I had come quickly in—not knowing she was there—disoriented, with a long tear in my nightgown and scarlet welts around my neck.

I let out a rush of breath when I saw her.

"E. Jean!" whispered C. C.

It was strange for me to hear C. C.—Cynthia Cruickshank Dyer, whose voice is louder than a howler monkey and whose hair is redder than wild tomato—*whisper*. C. C. is a TV producer. The rip in the nightgown, the burst blood vessels in my eyes, the marks around my neck, revealed to her the truth in about half a second.

"You're hurt," she whispered.

She was whispering because the *last* thing either of us wanted to do was wake Geraldo and have *him* come lumbering downstairs.

"Naw," I whispered. "J. J. and I just had a . . . tussle."

"Should I call the—" She never finished the sentence.

I cut her off. "Naw, naw. I'm fine!"

And indeed, when this tussle was happening upstairs, with Geraldo and C. C. supposedly both fast asleep in the bedroom next door, J. J., who is six foot three and was in a rage because I'd called him an "ape," was kneeling on the bed, bending me to one side on the mattress, tightening his hands around my neck, crushing my windpipe, strangling me in silence. In silence! Probably most strangling goes on in silence, now that I think about it. Not total silence—I could hear the sounds of the sheets moving ferociously under his knees and his breathing, which was choppy, like he was competing in a set of tennis. I *knew* I was being strangled, rather than feeling it. I kept smashing him hard in the ear with my fist. It loosened his grip. I broke away. He grabbed me again. I kicked. He ripped the nightgown. I ran downstairs.

4

Geraldo (bless him!) slept through the whole thing, and till I see the woman with the red ponytail in Anita, Indiana—the exact red of C. C.'s hair—I hadn't remembered the incident in years.

"Do you have a room with a microwave?" I ask the motel clerk.

"Yes, I'm giving you a room with a very *good* microwave."

"Excellent," I say. "And one more question . . ."

The motel clerk encodes one of the white plastic room cards with a swipe, hands it to me, and raises her sandy eyebrows with curiosity.

"I've been wondering," I say.

"What about?" says the motel clerk, thinking probably I'm about to ask if the room has a refrigerator.

"What Do We Need Men For?" I say.

She hoots.

"Nothing," she says.

"ABSOLUTELY NOTHING!" comes a voice from the sofa.

When J. J. was strangling me, this is the time on the stairway, not on the bed, and I had *almost* gotten away and was calculating if I could make it to the nearest phone to call the sheriff before J. J. killed me, and he got me again from the back, I just want to point out so you will know precisely what kind of man I am talking about, Ladies, so you will know exactly what kind of man is entertaining us all here in this book by shutting down my windpipe, that J. J.'s framed awards, accolades, honors, citations, plaques, Emmy tributes, etc., etc., were hanging all the way up the stairway beside us.

I was a writer at *Saturday Night Live.** There are great writers at *SNL,* there are good writers at *SNL,* there are bad writers at *SNL,* there are very bad writers at *SNL,* there are really very bad writers at *SNL,* and then there was E. Jean. The worst. This was, I think, in 1986/87—I had to Google it—and one Thursday night, I was, as usual, at Elaine's, the fabled restaurant where writers and actors so packed the place that Elaine once threw out a woman sitting with Norman Mailer for unscrewing a lightbulb. ("Listen, sweetheart," says Elaine. "Get your ass outta here. *Him* I have to take it from, but no half-a-hooker is gonna fuck with my lightbulbs!") I was sitting at the "regulars" table (magazine people, detectives, TV writers, prizefighters, etc.), and I'd brought along Prince Solomon Habte-Selassie of the royal family

---

* I worked with Al Franken, who was the *least* pervy guy in New York. What the Democrats were thinking when they made him leave the US Senate is beyond me.

of Ethiopia, whose members trace their ancestry back to King Solomon of Israel and the Queen of Sheba.

Now, Ladies, I had met the prince when I was doing a story about fraternities at Dartmouth for *Playboy* (a story, by the by, which the alumnae furiously tried to spike), and the prince was one of the handsomest young chaps you ever saw. But when J. J., the big-time New York anchorman, and one of the prettiest and most accomplished men in Manhattan, who was sitting at *his* usual table with Geraldo, pushed back his chair at one end of Elaine's, and when it so happened that I pushed back my chair at the other end of Elaine's at the same moment, and when it also happened that we looked at one another, well, Ladies, that was it. IT. In capital letters. J. J. followed me out of Elaine's that night, bowed like Lord Chesterfield to Prince Solomon, and asked for my number.

Later, another night over margaritas, Geraldo, who was about to begin his eleven-year run with the *Geraldo* show, and who was/is—bizarrely—an attorney, wrote our prenup on a cocktail napkin.

"If we divorce, I don't want a fucking dishcloth!" I said. "Write *that,* Geraldo!"

C. C. and one of the waiters witnessed and signed it. Had Elizabeth Gilbert and her first husband done this, their divorce would have gone more smoothly, Miss Liz would not have ended up weeping on the bathroom floor, and the wonderful *Eat, Pray, Love* would never have been written. So I hesitate to recommend The Cocktail Napkin Prenup to memoir writers.

C. C., a woman of action, as are all redheads (when Geraldo came home late one night, she said she swung on him and knocked his front tooth out of his head with such force that it flew across the entrance hall), baked one of her famous strawberry-rhubarb pies, and when J. J. and I ran away and got married in the Hamptons, C. C. and Geraldo were our best man and best woman.

C. C. and me, and, yes, this photo is blurry because we are dancing.

My God! We were *fabulous!* We had scenes all over the Carib-
bean! One time when J. J. was being particularly blustery, I
picked up a suitcase and bashed him over the head with it. Another time, shortly after the Stairway to Heaven incident, I
waited for him to leave the house to catch his plane for St. Barts.
I then packed up every personal item I owned, put Hepburn de
Balzac and Tits, the dogs, into the car, and left our house, which
was once owned by Kurt Weill and his wife, Lotte Lenya. Weill,
of course, wrote "Mack the Knife" and *The Threepenny Opera*—
little did he imagine such bloodcurdling screeching coming from
his living room! Miss Lotte was the celebrated singer and actress,
the SPECTRE agent in *From Russia with Love* who nearly kills
James Bond with a poisoned switchblade hidden in her shoe. But
I left these famous digs and moved into even more famous digs—
Helen Hayes (the "First Lady of American Theater," one of only
fifteen people to win an Oscar, Emmy, Grammy, and Tony) had

a famous old farmhouse with a stunning stone grain silo. I rented it for $650 a month. And, no, I didn't take so much as a dish-cloth.*

So I understand the woman with the ponytail who said, "I'll give him whatever he wants! I want out!"

6 ·········▶

1. Hang Do Not Disturb sign outside motel room door.
2. Open windows.
3. Close curtains.
4. Unplug room phones.
5. Unplug room alarm clocks.
6. Unplug lamp and drag to other side of bed.
7. Move desk under window.
8. Place large bath towel over desk chair, and, without touching back, seat, or arms, move it across room to the desk.
9. Clorox-wipe TV remote.
10. Clorox-wipe sink faucet handles, shower knobs, toilet-flusher handle, light switches, front door handle, closet handles, microwave buttons.
11. Wash out ice container and fill with water for Lewis Carroll.

---

* J. J. has apologized four or five times for his past behavior.

12. Leave big tip for housekeeper, who must drag everything back where it belongs after we leave.*

You see #9 and #10 on the list? *Other* women might be frightened of men—it's always a man—hiding in their closets or under their motel beds with a butcher knife, ready to cut them up and send them in a trunk to New Jersey. Not me. Just show me a Clorox wipe and a bathroom light switch that I don't dare touch, and I'm good. And please don't think I'm a germophobe.

Am I the woman who walked from Telefomin, across the Star Mountains of Papua New Guinea straight through two warring tribes to the border of Irian Jaya with only Bikki, an Atbalman warrior, and Sali, the son of the Telefomin Big Man, as my guides, ate off the ground, and did not change clothes or bathe for six weeks? *Yes, I am that woman.* So, no, I happen to *like* germs. I was on that little New Guinea caper, by the way, because I'd begged Jim Morgan, my editor, to send me there to "find primitive man."

Like many women of the 1980s, I had grown sick of modern men and their sniveling. So I bought a pair of jungle boots issued by the US Army—and here I doff my wig to the great Cheryl

---

* It is a well-known fact that the sperm count of American men has dropped 50 percent in the last forty years. I can tell you where the other 50 percent of the sperm reside. By the simple method of covering the flash on my iPhone with Scotch tape, coloring the piece tape with a blue Sharpie, putting *another* piece of tape on top of the blue tape, and coloring *that* with a purple Sharpie, I can turn my cell phone into UV light and can see the sperm glowing like Madame Curie's radioactive nail polish.

Ladies: Listen to your advice columnist. NEVER REMOVE YOUR SHOES IN A HARDWICK INN.

Lewis Carroll and I follow precautions 1 through 12 as we enter our Hardwick Inn and Suites room after receiving our key card from the sandy-haired desk clerk.

Now, Ladies, confess. You think I'm taking this sperm thing a bit far with #8. Item #8 is not pleasant for you. And very far from pleasant to me, but I urge you, when traveling, to find the biggest towel on offer in the bathroom and place it over the desk chair before sitting in or moving that bugger. Why?

I don't need to point out that the *desk chair* is where the male of the species sits with his apparatus of happiness and watches porn on his laptop while galloping his antelope, do I?

Strayed, who was smart enough to purchase *her* boots at REI for her famous 1,100-mile Pacific Crest Trail walk—what a woman! What a writer! Hi, Cheryl!—and I *did* find the primitive chap I was looking for. He was so far back and so high up in the Star Mountains, he gave me a stone ax as a present. I gave him my cornflower-blue cross-country ski socks. He was a very good-looking chap—an artist of the forest, quiet, lean, four foot two, wearing a penis gourd and quills through his nose.

This microwave *is* working quite well, I must say!

In the Star Mountains of Papua New Guinea, 1984. I had never lingered with people who had not before encountered uncivilized, noisy, twentieth-century specimens like me. I gave them bars of soap, shared a meal, and Sali, Bikki, and I moved on!

The Anita, Indiana, Whiny Dick Hour approaches.

Lewis Carroll has enjoyed his bowl of Rachael Ray dog food. I have dispatched my Amy's Organic Cheddar Cheese, Bean & Rice Burrito mixed with one can of Amy's Organic Chili with Vegetables (spicy), and finished off with two Strawberry Halo Tops (made by Eden Dairy . . . Eden, as I've mentioned in the modest prologue, is the #131 most popular girl's name), and now I fluff up *all* the pillows on the bed (after carefully removing the bedspread with my pliers—the sperm counts in American hotels being, as I have mentioned in that long footnote, so disagreeably high, a lady is compelled to provide herself with kitchen tongs or pliers or grappling hooks—and hurling it to the floor), and we may, at last, settle in for the *Whiny Dick Hour.*

This is when, constantly asking, "What Do We Need Men For?" I refresh my browser every fifteen seconds to read the headlines on *The New York Times, The Washington Post, The New Yorker,* etc., and see which famous new chump has locked his office door and banged *his* female assistant from behind until she fainted, and who is now "coming forward" to whine an apology.

I think it is agreed by all parties that the melancholy object Harvey Weinstein represents the deplorable state of men in America. In fact, Ladies, the whining of Harvey Weinstein is causing me to reconsider whether we have *over*estimated the value of his personal sulfur, potassium, calcium, and nitrogen, and *under*estimated his personal carbon. Indeed, I believe the man's carbon will bring us twice what we expected.

Read this transcript of Weinstein, who looks like he's been stuffed by an inebriated taxidermist, begging the young Filipina-Italian model and actress Ambra Battilana Gutierrez, whose breasts he mauled the day before, to come inside his hotel room and watch him shower. The audio of the video was posted online by *The New Yorker,* in a breaking story written by Mia Farrow's son Ronan Farrow. Here is a shortened version:

Weinstein: I'm telling you right now, get in here.

Gutierrez: What do we have to do here?

Weinstein: Nothing. I'm going to take a shower, you sit there and have a drink.

Gutierrez: No.

Weinstein: Please?

Gutierrez: No, yesterday was kind of aggressive for me.

Weinstein: I know—

Gutierrez: I need to know a person to be touched.

Weinstein: I won't do a thing, please. I swear I won't. Just sit with me. Don't embarrass me in the hotel. I'm here all the time. Sit with me, I promise—

Gutierrez: Please, I don't want to do something I don't want to.

Weinstein: I won't do anything and you'll never see me again after this. OK? That's it. If you don't—if you embarrass me in this hotel where I'm staying—

Gutierrez: It's just that I don't feel comfortable.

Weinstein: Please. I'm not gonna do anything. I swear on my children. Please come in. On everything. I'm a famous guy.

Gutierrez: Why yesterday you touch my breast?

Weinstein: Oh, please. I'm sorry. Just come on in. I'm used to that.

Gutierrez: You're used to that?

Weinstein: Yes, come in.

Gutierrez: No, but I'm not used to that.

Weinstein: Don't ruin your friendship with me for five minutes.

Gutierrez: I know—but, it's kind of, like, it's too much for me. I can't.

Weinstein: Please, you're making a big scene here. Please.

Gutierrez: No, but I wanna leave.

Weinstein: OK, bye. Thank you.

Ladies, a woman breathes in oxygen (O) and expels carbon dioxide (CO_2). But a man like Harvey Weinstein? As you see from the above, he does not breathe in or out. He *whines*. And why does he whine? Because of his high carbon content. So here is another great advantage of my scheme. Not only will we be clearing America of the male nuisance and their interminable farting and whining, we will be eliminating a high percentage of greenhouse gases.

And now, Ladies, I must wish you good night.

IV

"She's . . . Uh, Having Boy Problems Right Now."

Bonnie, Illinois
(#1,266 Most Popular Girl's Name)

"Yes! I want some of them famous Bonnie Café scrambled eggs with onions and tomatoes, and a stack of whole-wheat toast with triple butter, and strawberry jelly, and coffee, and a side of them french fries, and a side of that taco salad with extra cheddar, and a slice of the butter pecan cake à la mode, and a side of macaroni and cheese for Lewis, and a bottle of Guinness—oh, no Guinness? And so you're having boy problems, huh?" I say to Jaklyn and Hannah, two college girls I meet in the Bonnie Café.

The girls smile gloomily at one another over their eggs and hash.

I meet them when I stop by their table, and, leaning down, announce to Jaklyn, "WOW, are you Scottish!" and Jaklyn says she is not Scottish, and I tell her she *is* Scottish, and Jaklyn says, no, she is *not* Scottish, and I say, yes, she is Scottish, because nobody with hair that fabulous rusty-red color is *not* Scottish and ask Jaklyn to tell me what her last name is—and, of course—it is Scottish, and I inquire if I may join them.

Jaklyn is eighteen, has an academic scholarship, and is majoring in social work. Hannah, also eighteen, grew up in the same little Illinois town as Jaklyn, plays volleyball, majors in physical therapy, and is on an athletic scholarship.

"So what *is* the boy problem?" I say. "Who's the boy?"

The Bonnie Café, with its 4.8 stars out of 5 on Facebook, its roll of paper towels on each table, its soap opera on the TV, and its caustic, platinum-haired, philosopher-waitresses, is to Bonnie, Illinois, what the English coffeehouse was to seventeenth- and eighteenth-century London—the hub of gossip, fashion, scandal, and metaphysical debate upon deep subjects, and the two girls and I are in the mood to take this boy, whoever he is, put him on the slab, and dissect him.

But little do the young coeds dare suspect, they are sitting in the Bonnie Café with college royalty—a monarch, a crowned head, a Miss Indiana University. Yes, Ladies, cheerleading is one thing, queening is quite another. I was Emblem of All Sweater Sets, Joy and Terror of that hallowed institution—Queen of its thirty-two thousand students.

The former Miss Indiana University Linda Lou Mugg crowning your advice columnist, with Miss America Jacquelyn Mayer presenting the roses. Photo by the great Elinor Hendrix.

It was the talent portion, I believe, in which I hypnotized the judges. I took to the IU auditorium stage dressed as Edith Sitwell and performed a dramatic reading of a Dick and Jane book.

My sorority, Pi Beta Phi—Yes! Yes! I pledge Pi Phi! And just let me say here that the Pi Phi house, a white-columned mansion on Third Street in Bloomington, Indiana, directly across the street from the Kinsey Institute for Research in Sex, Gender, and Reproduction, produces at the time I'm talking about more beauty queens, homecoming queens, fraternity queens, Indy 500 queens, etc., etc., than any sorority in the state, probably the Midwest, and this is in the days when beauty queens *rule*—it's the Pi Phis who put me up for Miss Indiana University.

And, boy! Is your advice columnist *enthusiastic!* If the athletic department or my sorority decide to put me up for a championship, by God! I will don those scarlet-red cheerleader underpants!

Yes! I will squeeze into that swimsuit with the modesty panel and race up and down that runway like a cheetah chasing a baby gazelle.

Indeed, Ladies, beauty contests are such a rage when I am growing up that my Girl Scout camp—*my Girl Scout camp!*—holds yearly beauty pageants. So, it happens that the first beauty contest I am nominated for is Miss Camp Ella J. Logan. The year before I am put up, I watch Merle Baldwin, whom I worship with a love greater than Harriet Smith for Emma Woodhouse, win the Miss Camp Ella J. Logan Pageant. Even from a distance of sixty-three years, I see blond and laughing Merle—the best swimmer in camp!—shimmering up and down the dock on the Camp Ella J. Logan waterfront, pigeon-toed, tanned, and chuckling.

This camp, by the way, is in the piney woods of northern Indiana, and it forms, along with the movie *Dumbo* and *The Girl Scout Handbook*, my moral and ethical basis for living. Indeed, it is such a remarkable training ground for genius that Merle Baldwin goes on to become a Pi Beta Phi at Indiana. (I should also perhaps mention that Merle, the former Head of the International Atomic Energy Agency Office in Geneva, and a senior official of the IAEA in the area of Non-Proliferation Treaty negotiations, helps keep the world safe from 1967 to 2000, but we're only sticking to the important stuff here.)

The contestants in the Miss Camp Ella J. Logan beauty contest the year I am put up are as follows:

Miss Whistle Wind—a Brownie Scout
Miss Keewaden—an Intermediate Scout
Miss Wakada—a Scout
Miss Pioneer—a Senior Scout
Miss Kiwanis—Betty Jean Carroll

If they had *had* a talent portion, I would have demonstrated my knife-throwing, compass-reading, fire-building, broken-arm-setting, poem-reciting, pet-training, trail-blazing, knot-tying, or good-deed-doing ability. But after we walked up and down the dock, the judges, who have roared across the lake in a magnificent Chris-Craft, and who are seated in deck chairs, call my name.

I walk over and whisper:

"What?"

They whisper:

"You are Miss Camp Ella J. Logan."

After they put the papier-mâché crown on my head and the cape on my shoulders and give me the baton covered in Reynolds Wrap, Old Cam, **#6** on **The Most Hideous Men of My Life List,** the waterfront director, takes me out in a boat and runs his hands under my shirt and up my shorts.

He is breathing and moving his hand slowly and hotly, and I fight no battles in my head. My mind goes white. This is Cam. This is the man who has watched me grow from an eight-year-old Brownie Scout when I first came to camp, and his notice is an honor. This is Cam, who teaches me to swim and dive, and awards me the coveted White Cap! This is Cam, who continues to run his hand inside my shorts and under my blouse—even in the dining room during dinner, under the table, squeezing my thighs, shoving his fingers—saying, "You're my girl. You're my

girl. You're my girl," and making me promise "not to tell anyone." He does this until I go home. I am twelve.

My friends will be stunned to read this. My sisters and brother
will be speechless. But Aly Raisman, the great Olympian gym-
nast, and the 150 young women who spoke out in court about
Lawrence Nassar, the USA gymnastics team doctor, will not be
shocked. Nassar abused some of the young women in front of
their own mothers. Nobody saw it.

And old Cam? He writes a book called *The Girl Scout Man*. It
is listed in "rather remarkable" condition, though there is some
"light foxing and some very modest yellowing of the pages," on
Abe Books, the rare books dealer. Here is a shortened version of
its description:

> This loving homage to Girl Scouting is a record of many of the
> experiences and incidents and occurrences spanning the over
> twenty-five years of dedicated service of Cam and Brownie
> Parks, done mostly at Camp Ella J. Logan, near Fort Wayne,
> Indiana, on the shore of Dewart Lake. Cam was the longtime
> waterfront director at Camp Logan, his main duties being to
> provide instruction in swimming, diving, boating, canoeing,
> and Junior and Senior Lifesaving courses, as well as doing mi-
> nor repairs and other miscellaneous tasks that needed doing
> around camp. If you, Reader, are an alumnus of Logan . . . If
> you're reading this, memories of time spent at this camp may
> well be sweeping over you right now. . . .

No, thank you. The *last* thing I need are more "memories" of
time spent at camp "sweeping over" me. God! I have the most
terrible backache! I knew I was going to write about Camp Ella
J. Logan today, and the backache is growing, growing, growing
so badly I can't stand up. As a Scout, I returned to Camp Ella J.
Logan year after year, growing tall and womanly, receiving letters from boys with *SWAK* written on the backs of the enve-

lopes, going on weeklong canoe trips, and completing my counselor-in-training program.

Cam, I avoided. Never once did I speak to him or look at him, but my brain does not avoid him. He and his maroon swim trunks may have been dead these last forty years, but old Cam and the boat are the events—of all the events in my life—that somehow swim constantly back into my head, bearing me back, as Fitzgerald said, "ceaselessly into the past." The other events I mention here rarely enter my mind. That changes, naturally, at 2:47 A.M., November 9, 2016, the moment, in Lisa Birnbach's living room, we watch Donald Trump declared president.

"I try to keep calm, but I can't," says young Jaklyn, the college student and Scots denier in the Bonnie Café.

"So what's the boy doing that makes you mad?" I say.

"Bad things."

"Well . . ." I say. I pause and consider her.

I can see that she is off her oats about him, and I hadn't had any luck raising her spirits by asking "What Do We Need Men For?" and her answering with a laugh and a shake of the head. But I believe every young woman starting out in life ought to know the truth about coping with a dickwad.

"So . . ." I say. "Because he's doing bad things. Because you are eighteen years old. Because you are gorgeous and don't want to waste the golden hours of your youth on a dipshit . . . I advise you to leave him in the dust!"

This seems to strike the proper note.

"I could! That's true!" she says, glancing around the Bonnie Café like she's Mary, Queen of Scots, deciding to flee the Earl of Bothwell.

"Have you got the chap's picture?" I say.

She pulls up a boy on her phone and pushes it in my direction so I can see. I pull it closer.

I enlarge it.

"DAMN!!"

Jaklyn bursts into happy laughter, and Hannah's eyebrows, which are drawn on with a pencil like an old lady's—wild and swaggering—shoot up with pride that her best friend's boyfriend is hotter than a fritter.

"He's so handsome," I say.

The lad is doing The Dickwad Pose—hat on backward, tongue stuck out, six-pack declaring war on North Korea.

"He's not treating you too well?" I say.

"He's a good guy," says Jaklyn. "He's just trying to move too fast."

"You know," I say. "There's a lesson every woman should learn her freshman year in college."

"What?"

They lean forward over their plates.

"You're only on this earth," I say, "for one reason."

"What?" says Hannah, lowering her magnificent eyebrows.

"To enjoy as many chaps as you can," I say.

[Silence.]

I don't think they understand me. I throw my arms open.

"As many guys as you like!" I cry.

Their eyes light up, but it's probably because one of the waitresses, either Miss Nikki, who says she doesn't need a man for "anything except sex," or Miss I-Didn't-Get-Her-Name, both of whom should be in the US Senate and have been bringing us plate after plate, and now one of them leaves the checks on the table, and I snatch up both bills, saying, "Lunch is on me!"

Lewis Carroll, who is waiting in Miss Bingley, and who expects me to exit every diner carrying a doggie bag, spots the container of mac and cheese when I am three steps out the door and glues his eyes to it as I toddle across the jammed Bonnie Café parking lot.

"Look what I have, Lewis!" I sing out.

Lewis is a very tidy dog. He does not like food cluttering up Miss Bingley, and he cleans out that container of mac and cheese like Marie Kondo going after a sock drawer.

Ladies! My backache is gone! I am imagining all the queen-hell possibilities open for our two college girls, and thinking back to *my* first boyfriend, Lyle—Lyle in the cowboy shirt (of course!) in the first row to the far left. Your advice columnist is in the middle of the second row with the light dress, puffy sleeves, and hair bow (of course).

Huntertown, Indiana, grade school. Miss Newland was our teacher and a marvel!

V

"I've Showed It to a Lot of People, but Nobody Can Tell Me What It Is."

Ina, Illinois
(#1,732 Most Popular Girl's Name)

1 ···········▶

DEAR E. JEAN: Where do you go to meet rich men? (I'm asking for a friend.)—*Indispensable**

INDISPENSABLE, MY KUMQUAT: Here are E. Jean's Twelve Places To Meet a Rich Man:

1. The Yale Club is better than the country club.
2. The country club is better than "Hair Club" for Men.
3. The trust-funder wedding is better than the golf course.
4. The charity ball is better than the yacht race.
5. The yacht race is better than the museum gala.
6. The polo match is better than the fine antiques auction.
7. The Sun Valley Mogul Summer Camp is better than the Henley Regatta.
8. The private box is better than the orchestra.
9. The private suite at the Lakers game is better than the private suite at the Knicks game.
10. The private island is better than any island except for the Island of Manhattan.
11. The private airport is better than the private island.
12. The private plane at the private airport is better than anywhere!

* From the March 2013 *Elle*.

Ladies, there is not a rich man in sight. It is a pale, blue, blustery What Do We Need Men For day. The road from Bonnie, Illinois, to Ina, Illinois, is flat as a mud flap and dusty as an ugly man's dancing shoes. Despite the wind, a Midwest languor loafs over the fields. Lewis is standing up in the back seat and leaning his head over my shoulder, aiming his brown-eyed stare through Miss Bingley's windshield. In his golden years, his high beams aren't quite as sharp, but he can still spot the death by defenestration of a half-eaten Burger King thirty yards ahead on the road.

Indeed, great are the advantages of traveling with Lewis. He doesn't change the song. He *likes* gas station ladies' rooms. He doesn't forget his phone charger and makes one turn around and drives fourteen miles back to the motel to retrieve it. He doesn't drop his credit card between the seats. He doesn't go off his gourd when a wolf spider drops from the car ceiling. He doesn't argue about directions. He doesn't cut in line at Dairy Queen. He doesn't stop at historical markers commemorating white males. He doesn't Instagram a photo of one when one has to stop and squat behind a bush on the side of the road. He doesn't party in the back seat until after two in the afternoon.

"We came out on this trip to ask people What Do We Need Men For," I say aloud. "And if it happens that we don't need men for anything, well, we have an excellent plan for getting rid of them. Right?"

Lewis looks into my right ear and clicks his teeth.

"Clak-clak-clak-clak."

This means he is listening.

"But we forgot a major detail," I say. "Some chaps are rich. Who inherits their money when we sell their elements?"

"Clak-clak-clak-clak."

"Do women get the money?" I say.

[Silence.]

"Lewis, are you listening?"

"Clak-clak."

"Women get the rich guys' money? Right?"

"Clak-clak-clak-clak."

"Getting the money won't make us look greedy, will it?" I say. "Men *owe* us restitution! Right? No one could be more innocent than we women. No one's motives could be purer. If we find out we don't need men, we get rid of them—rich and poor alike. Right? What could be more fair? Take the male members of the president's cabinet, for instance. Many of them are billionaires. We will not discriminate. We will do away with the billionaires in the cabinet as we do away with the millionaires in the cabinet, right? I ask you, Lewis, who could be more fair and square than women?"

I like talking to Lewis. He doesn't interrupt except to turn around four or five times, drop his head on his paws, and go to sleep.

Are there men in possession of large fortunes in Ina, Illinois? For every 100 females in Ina, there are 1,082 males. Ina is right off Route 37. We can't miss Ina, Ladies! The towers of the Big Muddy River Correctional Center will let us know we've arrived.

I am shopping the beautiful leg irons and the—talk about seren-dipity!—wind-up teeth, which are in excellent working condi-tion, when I spy the *real* treasure, which is behind the counter of Ina Antiques & Collectibles and placed on top of the Harley Davidson floor mat by Bryce Heard, proprietor.

"Oh!" I exclaim. "What is it?"

"You tell me," says Mr. Heard.

I glance at Mr. Sheridan, who was no doubt voted cutest boy in his class, and Mr. Hogan, two friends of Mr. Heard, the three chaps—not a one of them under seventy—making up the Holy Trinity of former male power in Ina. Mr. Hogan's actual name I can't tell you, but he has a horseshoe mustache and long white hair like Hulk Hogan, the legendary wrestler, and when I had asked him his name, he had looked off into the distance, trying, with great effort, to recall it, and the lads had started laughing, with Mr. Hogan hee-hawing, the most delighted of the three.

As for grilling them with, "What Do We Need Men For?" forget it. They had answered:

"So our wives will have somebody to boss around."

In other words, they had answered what all men who are 100 percent sure women are not the boss and have never been the boss have been answering for the last twelve thousand years. But now, the three lads are silent and waiting with anticipation as I bend closer over the counter to look at the mysterious object.

Ladies, do you like rich men?

I was raised in a redbrick schoolhouse, deep in the hills outside Huntertown, Indiana. Across the road was a redbrick church with a steeple.

My childhood house. In the photograph, which was taken near the close of
the nineteenth century, you can see—in the bell tower—the bell. The rope to
ring it hung down through the roof into the "coatroom." I would climb and
swing on that rope like Quasimodo. In fact, I rang the bell so much the rope
broke.

Across from the church was a graveyard where I and my
boxer dog, Heidi, hid inside the new-dug graves, waiting to surprise the mourners. Behind the graveyard was a hill that Heidi
and I ran up and down. The big hill on the other side of the road,
beside the church, Heidi and I avoided because the prize bull,
whose semen was so famous that he made more money in a year
than my father, once chased us all the way . . . *to the fence!*

I was such a rich child that one day I abandoned this bucolic
splendor, left Heidi, the goat, the cat, the sheep, and the chickens
behind as decoys, sneaked out of the house, and, with money—a
fortune!—in my pocket and the wild idea of "going to the store,"
set out on my first shopping spree.

I was forced to return.

My mother met me at the door.

"What's the matter, Jeanie?"

"The sawmill dog barked at me."

"You're going to let the Garmans' dog *scarrrrrrrrrre* you," said my mother.

"No," I said. And I hung my head.

"Well . . ." said my mother. "How can you run away if you keep coming back?"

And, holding Heidi inside, she shut the door!

You either grow up to be a wimp with a mother like this or a hardnose who never gives up. I grew up to be both. I avoid *all* confrontations and joke my way through. Then I boil my brain for weeks and dream up revenge so delicious that the person I was afraid to confront in the first place comes over to my side and becomes (for a time) my best pal.

My mother closed the door. I turned around, and, dragging my feet in their red sandals with silver buckles, and looking back just once, and then about 157 more times, I crossed the yard and started up the dirt road again. The gravel was powdery, the air was hot, the sun was high, the route was lonely. I had a mile to go.

Have you ever pondered beauty, Ladies? I have, and it is a plastic ring with a compass inside of it, but not even a real compass, a compass *painted* on the inside of it. And, Ladies, I braved that sawmill dog who came rushing out from under the lilacs like the Hound of the Baskervilles, and I kept on walking! Yeee gods! What a shopper I was! How wealthy I thought myself! And here's the best part: I was four years old.*

---

* It is alarming to hear of a mother today sending a four-year-old girl down an *aisle* of a store unaccompanied, let alone sending her a mile down a deserted dirt road. But remember, Ladies, I was born during World War II. Kids who were raised in the 1940s were given just waaaaaay more independence, walked to school alone at age six, rode bikes all over town at nine or ten, and started driving cars at twelve or thirteen. Dad put me behind the wheel when I was twelve. We boomed along old US Highway 27 on the way up to Clear Lake, the whole family shouting encouragement as I tromped the accelerator to forty-nine miles per hour.

[*Note:* I realize this is nothing compared with the glittering Jeannette Walls and her *Glass Castle* childhood when she was cooking her own meals over the stove at age three and setting fire to herself and the family house. I worked with Jeannette at *Esquire* in the '90s, and I can tell you that Jeannette is *stupendous!* Brilliant, witty, six feet tall, always shod in the highest heels possible, garbed in the most perfectly cut suits in slate gray and dove blue, with that extraordinary mane of auburn-red hair, a jawline like a bank door, and charming hillbilly accent! What a woman!]

Ma, me, and Pan the goat—about the time I walked to the store.

I met my first rich boy in a tent on a family camping trip when I was five. I met my last rich boy in a dressing room of Bergdorf's when I was fifty-two.

My first rich boy pulled down my underpants. My last rich boy pulled down my tights.

My first rich boy—I had fixed my eyes on his face long enough to know—was beautiful, with dark gray eyes and long golden brown hair across his forehead. I don't know what he grew up to be. My last rich boy was blond. He grew up to be President.

The first rich boy's name was James. He was raped by his grandfather. He was raped by his uncles. He was beaten by his father. I don't know the particulars. My mother told me the stories much later. When he was six, he was taken away from his father and given to a rich couple, Arthur and Evelyn. Arthur and Evelyn were best friends with my parents.

One day, my parents gave a party. All the invited parents brought their kids. Arthur and Evelyn drove up from Indianapolis and brought James. The parents drank cocktails in the yard of the redbrick schoolhouse. The kids played up on the hill beside the schoolhouse. James was seven and a half or eight, a bloodthirsty, beautiful, relentless boy. He ordered everyone around. Even the older kids did what he commanded. To me, he said, "I'm going to shove this up you again."

I don't remember what it was that he was going to shove up me again, probably a stick. Or maybe it was a rock. But I remembered we'd played this game before. Our families had gone on the camping trip together to Pokagon State Park, and I learned that an object could be shoved up the place where I tinkled. It felt like being cut with a knife.

"I don't want to," I said.

We were standing on the hill. James looked at me for a moment with his feral gray eyes.

Then he wadded up a piece of fabric—I can't recall what it was—perhaps he took something from one of the other kids; I remember the color of it—it was a light blue-violet shade and looked fluffy, like a wadded-up hairnet kind of thing.

"Put this in your underpants," he said.

He pulled up my dress and crammed the bunched-up material down my pants. "You're bleeding," he said.

Late at night when the guests had gone home and I took off my dress, I pulled down my pants. And there it still was, the wadded-up thing.

11

James and I played so many ferocious games when we were camping that summer—hooking one another with fishhooks, tying one another up, striking one another with arrows, holding one another underwater, chasing one another with garter snakes, dumping hot embers from the fire on each other's heads, etc., etc.—the thing that James "shoved up" me has been lost in the shuffle of my memory. As for **The Most Hideous Men of My Life List,** that is for James to decide. It is his uncles, his father, his grandfather who should be recorded.

The summer of James.

"Nobody knows what it is," says Bryce Heard, proprietor of Ina Antiques & Collectibles.

"Mmmmmm," I say, turning the mysterious object round and round.

"It's been fashioned—made by hand, as you see," says Mr. Heard. "I've showed it to a lot of people, but nobody can tell me what it is."

"It's marvelous!" I say.

"Tremendous!" says Mr. Sheridan.

"It looks like a Venus figure," I say. "A fertility charm, or perhaps it is a self-portrait by a female artist." I don't mention to the chaps that I once heard an anthropologist whom I met in the Sydney airport call these little statuettes a very rude name.

"Send me a text," says Mr. Heard, "if you figure it out."

Ladies, it is a smooth, small (two inches wide, three inches long) carved brown stone whittled to reveal what look like two haunches and an orifice. Send an email to E.Jean@AskEJean.com, and I will reply with a photo.

Lewis and Miss Bingley being transported out of Pocahontas, Missouri.

VI

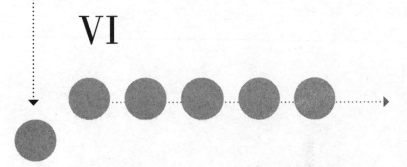

"I'm Reporting You to the Queen Committee!"

Jennette, Arkansas
(#5,360 Most Popular Girl's Name)

Blytheville, Arkansas
 (#1,623 Most Popular Girl's Name)

Pocahontas, Missouri
 (#8,880 Most Popular Girl's Name)

Warning: Ladies, this chapter contains the distressing history of men's abuse of Miss Bingley. If your car has experienced abuse by a man, please, dear Ladies, proceed with caution and do not torment yourselves!

Hag
Hag
Hag
Hag
Hag
Hag
Hag
Hag
Hag
Hag
Hag
Hag
Queen!
Hag
Hag
Servant
Queen!
Hag
Hag
Jester
Hag
Hag
King

Jester
Hag
Hag
Hag
Hag
Queen!
Queen!
Hag
King
Jester
Duchess
Hag
Servant
Servant
Servant
Hag
Hag
Queen!
Duke
Jester
Princess!!!
Jester
Hag
Hag

This is your advice columnist at five years old. I am sitting in the back seat of our dark blue Buick Roadmaster assigning social rank to each car we pass on the road.

At the age of three, I begin ranking Cadillac Fleetwoods and Chrysler Royals as Queens. At three and a half, Pontiac Torpedos and Oldsmobile 98s as Kings. By age four, I am classing the latest-model Chevrolets, Mercuries, Dodges, Packards, DeSotos, Lincolns, Fords, and Plymouths as Duchesses and Dukes. And by five I am the Burke's Peerage of motorcars and dividing the *whooooooooosh whooooooooosh whooooooooosh* of oncoming traffic into Servants, Jesters, Hags, Princes, Princesses, Dukes, Duchesses, Kings, Queens.

Princesses (i.e., ruby, sapphire, and emerald convertibles) are my favorites. Sports cars are Princes. Station wagons and pickup trucks are Jesters. Old, ugly cars are Hags—hideous, awful, terrible objects, so I give them all sorts of magical powers, because, as I am ranking, I am making an odd discovery:

Fairy tales get it wrong. Wrong. Wrong.

Kings are idiots. Hags are the smartest, but they can't quite manage to take over and run things. It is Queens—*Queens!*—who rule.*

Even today, as we boom along on our What Do We Need Men For trip, I find myself absentmindedly social-ranking oncoming traffic.†

And people wonder why I never describe the countryside!

So, at any rate, Ladies, you may be certain that when I tell you that it is a long, low, dark, heavy, brown Duke that pulls into our redbrick schoolhouse driveway one rainy night when I am alone with the babysitter, it *is* a Duke, and not a Prince.

---

* I don't have a flying fig of an idea WHY I was so certain that the rigid caste system in fairy tales was wrong. Except for Hans Christian Andersen and Lewis Carroll, both of whom always made a very big deal over Queens, the status arrangement in the stories just *felt* off to me. Probably—and I'm guessing here—I was breathing the scent of the great wads of cash infusing every inch of Indiana just after the end of World War II, and women, I probably couldn't help noticing, were seizing their opportunities and beginning their unstinting rise. My mother, a feminist from her cradle, began her career in local Republican politics at this time.

WAIT! Can I footnote a footnote? My *formerly* Republican mother, and lifelong cat-lover, born before women could vote, asked for an absentee ballot so she could vote for Hillary Clinton for president. Two days later, she died, and my sister Barbie said, "Thank God she didn't live to see who won!"

† Though, I mean, Ladies, can *you* tell the difference between a $248,000 Maserati and a $17,599 Ford Fiesta? All cars these days look alike. Bah! Give me a Hag any day.

My parents are at a party. I am not in bed yet. The babysitter's boyfriend enters at **#7** on **The Most Hideous Men of My Life List,** raising his hands to his hair—the graceful gesture of an Indiana man checking his pompadour—and smiling at me. The babysitter claps her hands and cries, "Beddy-bye Time!" And we all march to my little bedroom, the babysitter, the boyfriend, and I, and the babysitter pulls off my pajama bottoms and spreads my legs as far as they will go, and the boyfriend fondles my guinea. Sometimes the babysitter and the boyfriend look around the little bedroom for objects to fondle my guinea with. They both lean over me, making magic passes over my guinea with a feather, and the babysitter who has pink pimples and the palest pink complexion and giant gray-blue eyes edged with long ashy-blond lashes watches my face with a worried expression and softly twiddles the feather on my guinea in a different direction. "What else can we try?" she whispers to her boyfriend, stumped.

My parents later fire the babysitter. Not for twiddling my guinea—which they do not know about, no matter how many times it happens—but because one night they come home from a party and I am wearing my snow boots at 1:30 A.M. The babysitter and her boyfriend, it turns out, have driven me in the big, brown Duke* *through an ice storm* all the way to Huntertown High School to celebrate an unexpected, practically staggering, win by the Huntertown Wildcats basketball team.

So, Ladies, the question we must debate is this:

On one side, we have Brendan Fraser, star of *The Mummy,* who tells reporter Zach Baron in GQ magazine that he attends a Hollywood Foreign Press Association luncheon at the Beverly Hills Hotel in 2003, and the former Hollywood Foreign Press Association president Philip Berk "grabs " his "ass cheek," and "one of his fingers" touches him "in the taint" and poor Mr. Brendan tells us he "feels ill" and that he "thinks" he is "going to cry," and this is one of the reasons, he says, he stops making movies for ten years.†

On the other side, you have a kid in a bed being fondled with a feather.

Who suffers more?

Brendan Fraser suffers more. The kid in the pajamas? *Naw.* I only suffer after I make funny comments about a big rich movie star's "ass cheek," and now I feel bad for *not* supporting the poor chap's "narrative of hurt."

---

* A Hudson with windows like a tank. It smelled of horsehair, and the seat felt pleasantly scratchy.

† Mr. Berk disputes Mr. Fraser's account. My God, even men deny men's stories.

Miss Bingley is a Queen.

Weighing 8,500 pounds at birth and made of hibiscus plants,* Miss Bingley is lounging on a used car lot in Hopatcong, New Jersey, dreaming of her faded youth, when Lewis jumps into her back seat and refuses to budge.

I pay $6,999 for her and fly in special automotive paint from California at a cost of $157.52, plus $199 for "anti-explosive shipping," and hand-paint—*hand-paint,* Ladies—blue polka dots and green frogs on her, as who, hailing from the state where the Indianapolis 500, "The Greatest Spectacle in Racing," is run, would not?

Miss Bingley is electric. Quiet as an eel in mud. Quiet as a feather in a pair of underpants. And so it is crazy that the very first day we set out on our What Do We Need Men For trip, I can *hear* her.

First it's just a little *ping ping ping ping.* Then it's a *jingle jingle jingle jingle* with a spot of *crank crank crank crank crank,* and now it is an extremely loud *screeeeeeeeeek screeeeeeeeeek screeeeeeeeeek,* and no matter how often Lewis and I stop to buy earplugs and shove them two and three together into our ears, no matter how much money I'm plunking down for noise-canceling headphones, no matter how many scarves I wrap around Lewis's head to keep the earplugs from falling out, and, no matter how many earplugs and

---

* Specifically, she is made of plant-based ecoplastics—kenaf, a member of the hibiscus family, and ramie, a nettle-family member—among other materials.

noise-canceling headphones I am wearing when I am talking with the mayor of Jennette, Arkansas, who pulls up beside me in his Jester, which is hauling a four-wheeler with a sprayer and raining down weed killer upon the road leading to Jennette, I can't hear a word of what *he* is saying, but *I can still hear Miss Bingley,* who by this time is bawling like a drunk at a Ted Nugent concert.

5

When I play the video of our interview later, I hear that the mayor, a handsome young chap of fifty in a DeFord Lumber cap, has had it up to *here* with men in the US Congress, men in the administration, men in most of the statehouses, and, to be blunt, men everywhere else, and his answer to "What Do We Need Men For?" is "We need men to *straighten up!* And do what they are *supposed* to do!"

John Mathis, mayor of Jennette.

6 ··········▶

As I can't find a female mechanic, I drive Miss Bingley, booming like she's setting off the cannons in Tchaikovsky's *1812 Overture*—registering 104–108 inner-ear-damaging decibels on my iPhone app—through the doors of Cleopatra Automotive, in Blytheville, Arkansas—Blytheville! A lady town!

Lewis and I are greeted by Ryan the owner, Danny the Mechanic, and Amber, the office manager.

Young Amber is engaged.

I ask to see her ring.

She holds out her hand with the smile of a woman who has found all earthly happiness.

"Beautiful!" I say. "What Do We Need Men For?"

"To take out the trash," says Amber.

It's Danny the Mechanic, sucking a straw stuck in a McDonald's Buttermilk Crispy Tenders cup the size of a Kotex can in a ladies' restroom, who warns me.

"I wish I had a camera," he says, "to videotape you when Ryan gives you the price of them wheel bearings and you fall over backward and your dog, Lewis, there has to catch you." Ladies, I will not trouble you with a particular account of our monetary negotiations.*

I will simply tell you that we conclude the bargaining with Lewis staring passionately into the giant Cleopatra Automotive fish tank and me clasping my hands together, raising my eyes to the heavens, and screaming, *"YEEEEEeeeeeeeeeeeeeeeeeeee gods!"*

---

* Suffice it to say that Danny the Mechanic gets eighty dollars an hour, and Miss Bingley's front two wheels will require 3.6 hours and the back 1.8, and what with Ryan wearing a neon-green shirt, and what with Danny the Mechanic getting ready to take the Bingley wheels *off* (and, as it will turn out, won't be putting them back on correctly), negotiations are *stirring!*

At the Blytheville Holiday Inn, I take a vacation from the *Whiny Dick Hour.*

I watch, instead, *The Center Will Not Hold,* the Joan Didion documentary on Netflix. She is a saint! She is an idol! But the remainder of the evening, I worry about Joan looking like she's been left out on the rocks and pecked clean by birds, and the next morning, Lewis and I return to Cleopatra Automotive. I pay $1,051.51 without quibbling, and, with one last glance at the fish tank, Lewis, looking spruce as Jay Gatsby with his hair slicked down, hops into the back seat, and, with Miss Bingley running silent as a submarine, we wave happy farewells to Ryan, Amber, and Danny the Mechanic, and blithely leave Blytheville.

Three hours later, a couple of miles outside Pocahontas, Missouri, Miss Bingley's brakes lock up like Catherine de' Medici's chastity belt, and, as Danny the Mechanic enters as **#8** on **The Most Hideous Men of My Life List,** we pirouette into a spin.

Luckily, we are on a back road and *already* slowing down because Miss Bingley is making such a racket *again,* and when her brakes go, after—let's be frank—a couple of lackluster half-twirls, all I have to do is slither her up an incline, and she rolls to a stop in a massive, empty parking lot.

Then I turn Miss Bingley off.

So much for the vehicle of my narration, eh, Ladies?

Pocahontas.* Pocahontas. Pocahontas. Pocahontas. Pocahontas. I am purling through my iPhone looking for the closest Toyota service place, when Stocky Man appears.

I can't tell you from where Stocky Man comes exactly; I don't see any vehicles. But he is a thick man, and he is walking toward me, looking at Miss Bingley with his small eyes, and says in a sharp, accusatory voice—like he's found me trying to take away his right to sell guns to criminals so they can shoot up a school:

"You can't park here."

I glance around the empty parking lot and smile up at him.

There is, as anyone who is rational can see, space for fifty or sixty cars. Or perhaps sixty-five cars, I mean, take a look at Google Street View. Don't you think sixty-five cars could fit in the

---

* A couple of hundred years ago, according to Sharon and Monte Penrod who run the delectable Pie Safe Bakery and Cafe in Pocahontas, a chap called Samuel Green—unable to pronounce or spell his Shawnee girlfriend's name—registers the town with the only native American princess name he *can* spell: Pocahontas.

I like to imagine the Shawnee girlfriend mounting her stallion, galloping out of Missouri, riding across America, founding her own town, and, because she can't keep white guys straight, calling it DermotMulroneyDylanMcDermottDeanMcDermott.

Semo Ag & Dairy parking lot, 2.3 miles south of Pocahontas, Missouri? Or do you think a mere sixty cars plus two trucks? What is your opinion, Ladies?

Lewis leans out his window.

Lewis doesn't need to sniff Stocky Man's personal trouser legs. Lewis can smell **#9** on **The Most Hideous Men of My Life List** twenty yards off.*

"The funniest thing just happened!" I say to Stocky Man, laughing and zooming my window all the way down like an idiot. "I just lost my brakes!"

Stocky Man's face, which is bloated and pale as a runny egg, turns red with irritation. Stocky Man is so irritated, in fact, the veins in his neck stand out like string cheese.

"*You can't park here,*" he says in a low rasp, rolling his shoulders and shoving his head forward.

"Oh!" I say jauntily, hitting the door locks and accidentally unlocking *all* the doors. "I won't be here long! Just going to call for a tow!"

Stocky Man steps closer.

He is dressed to sit in a duck blind. Not tall, but husky, with heavy shoulders and solid arms, topped with the bloated, runny-egg head with tiny eyes. I am not frightened of Stocky Man. I am seventy-five years old. I have lived too many adventures of this kind to be frightened, or, at least, let's say I am not *overly* frightened.

"You . . ." he says in a guttery, unnatural rasp, "*you* can't park here!"

"But I *can't* drive," I say. "My brakes just quit!"

"I don't care," he says. "Get out."

Is this the psychotic brother of the Get-the-Fuck-Out-of-

---

* I am as surprised and delighted as you are, Ladies, that some of the chumps we meet on the trip are making **The Hideous List**.

the-Middle-of-the-Fucking-Road-You-Fucking-Stupid-Cunt guy in Cynthiana, Indiana?

"I can't move the car!" I say. "The brakes don't work!"

Stocky Man leans forward, the better to bring his horrible little eyes closer to mine.

"Get out now," he says.

Ladies, do me a favor. Take a second glance at the Google Maps photos. Perhaps the place has changed owners, or perhaps Google has mislabeled it, but does this look like a *dairy* to you? One doesn't expect to see milkmaids with pails, but *come on!* Ladies, I don't know *what* it is, but I can tell you this:

At a time when all America is thirsting for advice, kicking an advice columnist with no brakes out of an empty parking lot indicates to me that Stocky Man and/or his people are up to no good.

I am not saying he is *absolutely* running the NRA's child porn operation, but without further ado, without asking Stocky Man "What Do We Need Men For," and suddenly feeling lucky to be escaping with my life and the certain knowledge that the whole male sex is so deranged that if we don't sell their elements soon, they'll destroy the planet, I roll in neutral with *no brakes* back down the incline onto Highway MO-C and down, down, down, down, down, thank God no cars are coming, down, down, down, down, down to Highway 61 and across to Huck Equine, the horse clinic, four hundred yards away. Here is where the celebrated and sweet-tempered veterinarian and horsewoman Dr. Martha Ann Huck-Miller practices, and here Miss Bingley lists, at last, to a stop.

I engage her parking brake and call for a tow to Coad Toyota in Cape Girardeau, Missouri.

In front of Huck Equine is a large statue of a bay horse. As a child growing up in the country, I ranked horses by color *viz:*

> White
> Palomino
> Black
> Paint
> Buckskin
> Sorrel
> Dapple gray
> Gray
> Chestnut
> Roan
> Bay

Now, you would think that my favorite horse color was white because I won an entire and complete Lone Ranger outfit[*] in a Cheerios contest when I was seven,[†] and because the Lone Ranger's horse, Silver, was white.

---

[*] I don't remember the dress I wore to my first prom, but I remember opening the huge box and drawing out by its black cuffs the beautiful embroidered buff-colored shirt, the black neckerchief, the golden bolo, the black trousers with buff piping and an embroidered cowgirl boot on each pocket, the very fine beaver hat with wind strap, the white holsters with leg ties, the long-barreled silver cap guns, the silver spurs, the three silver bullets in the belt, and the black mask.

[†] America was asked: "Why Do You Love Cheerios?" The winner received a white horse for his magnificent entry, "Because I can eat them with a toothpick." I came in second with "I love Cheerios because I can make breakfast by myself."

Indeed, you would think wrong, Ladies. My favorite horse color was white because *my* horse was white. My horse was on wheels and had a yellow mane, and I "galloped" my horse until I was quite worn out. I was three years old and I rode my horse upside down—turning him over on top of myself—and, as I "trotted" along, I received the greatest orgiastic thrills known to a human toddler.

You did this too, right, Ladies?*

A baby sex addict lying on the floor whooping it up with a wooden horse on top of her is not something that you want photojournalists from the Fort Wayne newspapers to see, however. So when my parents, Tom and Betty, who are young and full of

---

* I don't need to say that children enjoy many sexual adventures, and not all have to do with "abuse," do I?

beans, renovate the interior of the redbrick schoolhouse and put in a modern kitchen, bathroom, dining room, living room, and two bedrooms and the Fort Wayne *Journal Gazette* comes out to the country to photograph my mother, father, and me for a two-page spread, my mother makes certain that the white horse with the yellow mane is nowhere in sight, I promise you!

My parents, Tom and Betty, fell in love eating avocados at a roadside stand after a UCLA sorority ski trip to the mountains. I have had a yen for guacamole ever since.

This is the time of a million parties. Tom and Betty, though not in the first circle of Fort Wayne society, *viz* not Cadillacs or Chryslers . . . and though not in the second circle, *viz* not Olds-mobiles or Pontiacs . . . but solidly in the third (emerald convert-ibles!) are photographed quite often for the society pages, especially my ambitious, redheaded mother, and our redbrick schoolhouse, which is built in the Queen Ann style in 1888, is now listed (along with the graveyard and the late Gothic revival–style Salem Reformed Church across the road) on the National Register of Historic Places.

There are ice-skating parties, toboggan parties, wienie roasts, bridge parties, swimming parties, boating parties, cocktail par-ties, come-as-you-are parties, water-skiing parties, golfing par-ties, birthday parties, parties for visiting dignitaries, and dinner parties. The kids sometimes go to the parties, and when it gets dark, after filling us to the brim with potato chips and Cokes, our half-witted parents put us all in a bedroom, turn out the lights, and tell us to "go to sleep."

I remember the Wilsons' nineteenth-century farmhouse.

In the high-ceilinged living room, the dim adults are deco-rously drinking. In the bedroom, we kids are on a gaudy spree—dragging pillows off the beds, making tents out of the sheets and forts out of the chest of drawers, pulling the clothes off the hang-ers in the closets, and knocking over the knickknacks. The lights are off, but we can see one another in the glow of a golden bug light coming in through a window, and I am bouncing back and forth between the two beds, trying to evade a boy who is six or seven and whose stated aim in life is to tickle me "to death."

One of the older children, a well-grown girl of eleven or twelve, the ring leader, grabs the kid, says, "Leave Jeanie alone!" and twists his arm till he cries.

"Ha ha!" I say to the boy.

I am bouncing again on the bed to taunt him when the girl tells me to get off the bed, pull down my pants, and get on top of her.

She is lying on the floor.

I look down at her from the bed, fascinated.

"Why?" I say.

"Just wait! You'll see!"

Seven or eight kids, covered in potato chip droppings, stop what they are doing, interested in this new game.

The girl pulls down her own pants and stretches out again.

"Get on top of me," she says.

I get on top of her.

"No!" she says. "Take off your pants!"

I take off my pants.

"Get on me."

I climb on her.

"No!" she says. "Not like a toboggan. Like a sled."

"Hhhhhh?" I say.

"Like this—*lay out.*"

I lie on top of her, my feet out behind me.

She reaches her hand down to make certain her guinea is lined up with my guinea, and then she grips me by the shoulders—I am four years old and probably weigh, what? forty pounds?—and she pushes and pulls me up and down, up and down, up and down, up and down, up and down until—well, wouldn't you know! It is just as fun as my white horse.

We all take turns trying this new game until we are quite worn out and fall asleep; and, without waking up, we are carried in our fathers' arms out to the waiting Buick Roadmasters, the Chevrolet Fleetmasters, and the Studebaker Starlights and open our eyes the next morning in our own beds having dreamed of snow and riding the fastest sleds in Indiana.

Mauri Rose wins the Indianapolis 500 three times in the decade our dads carry us out to our cars, and I grow up ranking Indy crashes.

Number-One Crash: Two-time winner and reigning Indy champion Bill Vukovich, flying over the backfield retaining wall, somersaulting four and a half times and being decapitated.[*]

Number-Two Crash: Billy Arnold, defending Indy winner, breaking his rear axle, crashing into the wall, his tire soaring into the town of Speedway, Indiana, and landing on the head of Wilbur Brink, age eleven, who is playing in his backyard, killing him instantly, and so on.

The Indy 500 is the largest single-day sporting event in the world and is run at the Indianapolis Speedway, the largest sporting "facility" on earth. In the time I'm talking about here, Ladies, women are not allowed to drive in the Indy 500. Women are not allowed to walk on the track. Women are not even allowed to enter the pits.[†]

What *are* women allowed to do at the Indianapolis 500?

Women are allowed to reign as Queen or Princess.

There are thirty-three cars in the race and thirty-three Princesses. The Princesses attend the balls, appear on the floats in the

---

[*] This great driver wasn't decapitated. All us kids just liked saying he was.

[†] The pits are where the pit crews, wearing chic fireproof suits (I wore a geranium-red one last week to dine at Henry's with Robbie Myers), change the racing car's tires, add oil, etc. To see a pit stop, type "Indy 500 Pit Stop" into the YouTube search box.

parades, ride on the backs of the thirty-three official pace cars, and compete to be the Indianapolis 500 Queen and present the winner of the race with the famous bottle of milk.

It is 1963—nine years before Title IX centuples girls' and women's athletic competition. Consequently, the sport in which we women compete is the most deadly. The sport in which we compete is beauty pageants.

This year, because I am Miss Indiana University, I am asked to be one of the thirty-three Princesses vying to be Queen. I would prefer, of course, to drive *in* rather than reign *over* the race. For don't I speed the Smyth kids—Norine, Regan, Carla, and Robby, kids I am governessing during summers at Lake Geneva, Wisconsin—at no less than 115 miles an hour in the big banana cream–colored Ford convertible everywhere we go? Doesn't that same Ford engine do *very* well in NASCAR races? And isn't this also *another* good reason never to allow your child near a babysitter with a driver's license?

Standing with our hands over our hearts in the Royal Box of the Indianapolis 500 grandstand as the Purdue marching band plays "The Star-Spangled Banner," and then letting fall a shower of tears as Brian Sullivan, the opera singer (his body is found six years later floating in Lake Geneva, Switzerland, where he was the lead in *Götterdämmerung*), sings "Back Home Again in Indiana," we Princesses cheer Tony Hulman when he steps onto the track and says:

"Gentlemen! Start Your Engines!"

As far as I can remember, *viz,* with the help of *Wikipedia,* Parnelli Jones, in a red, white, and blue car nicknamed "Ol' Calhoun," is in pole position and leads lap 1 and possibly lap 2. Bobby Unser crashes into the wall on turn one in lap 3. Allen Crowe loses a wheel and crashes in lap 46. Smoke is seen coming from Parnelli Jones's engine in lap 80. Eddie Johnson spins like an eggbeater all the way down the back stretch and crashes in lap

120. Duane Carter explodes an engine in lap 160. Eddie Sachs hits the wall on turn three in lap 179. Eddie Sachs's pit crew calls for a black flag on Parnelli Jones, claiming Eddie crashes because Parnelli is leaking oil and smoke—excuse me, Ladies, I must quote bad language—"like a motherfucker." Roger McCluskey spins out and crashes in lap—HOLD IT!

Why am I driving up and down the country asking, "What Do We Need Men For?" It has just occurred to me, Ladies, that we can solve our problem of annoying men if we simply give every man in America a race car. What with the exploding and the spinning and the crashing, within seventy-two hours, there won't be a man left upright.

Let us think about this, Ladies.

And who takes the checkered flag? Parnelli Jones takes the checkered flag in the fastest Indy 500 race run to date.*

So now, Ladies, the only question, besides "Should we give every man in America a race car?" is the question of the milk. In one of racing's oldest traditions, the Queen steps into the winner's circle and presents the driver with a bottle of milk, which he chugs and pours on himself. (Will Power, one of the latest winners, breaks tradition and accidentally sprays it on the Queen, Miss Natalie Murdock, a fetching sophomore at Purdue University with a GPA of 3.72.) And so, does your advice columnist become Queen in 1963 and bestow upon Parnelli Jones the bottle of milk?

---

* *And* Parnelli Jones wins a fistfight the next day with Eddie Sachs.

Oh, and another question: How did **#8** on **The Most Hideous List,** Danny the Mechanic in Blytheville, Arkansas, cause your advice columnist to receive two black eyes and a broken nose 118 miles away in Cape Girardeau, Missouri?

Lewis Carroll, as we all recall with a shudder, reaches his personal low point when he accidentally smells the foul hide of **Hideous Man #9,** Stocky Man in Pocahontas, and if Lewis doesn't know a low point—wasn't Lewis born in a bad man's puppy mill? . . . didn't another bad man advertise Lewis as a "toy poodle"? . . . didn't Lewis, with his jaunty impudence, keep growing and growing and growing into a big standard poodle and consequently receive terrible thrashings by the man because not one, but *two* families *returned* him? . . . wasn't Lewis on the point of being "destroyed" when your advice columnist swooped in and took him home to her cabin in the Wawayanda Mountains, where, for the last twelve years, he has been splashing in the river and running up and down the Appalachian Trail kissing the hikers and humping the better-looking dogs?—if Lewis, as I say, doesn't know a low point, he will eat your size 8 shoe, Ladies!

And speaking of eating, a couple of days after we transport Miss Bingley to Coad Toyota to be fixed, I am heaping Lewis's plate with scrambled eggs, and since they don't have French toast for a French poodle, I am selecting the Belgian waffles from the free breakfast smorgasbord in the dining room of the Drury Lane Hotel, Cape Girardeau, where we are staying to be close to Miss Bingley, who is being fixed just down the road at the Toyota place.

I am about to take Lewis's plate up to him in our room, when I turn around, and, exactly as in a fairy tale, with the most unbounded, wonder-stricken surprise, who do I see sitting at a table in the Drury Lane Hotel dining area drinking coffee and eating jam and toast?

The Four Giantesses of Cape Girardeau!

They are magnificent, splendid, wonderful, rosy, beautiful, with arms as big as posthole diggers and thighs like bridge abutments.

"Ladies! Ladies! Ladies!" I exclaim joyfully.

The Four Giantesses, whom a sociologist would classify as "Missouri farm women," are a comely race—big, not fat—and they eye my Donna Karan kilt suspiciously.

"What Do We Need Men For?" I cry.

"Nothing," says the first Giantess.

"Nothing," says the second Giantess.

"Nothing," says the third Giantess.

"I *like* my husband!" says the fourth Giantess. "I can't give him up!"

This is a female, I remind you, who can pull a threshing machine *without a tractor.* Yet as an *Elle* fashion magazine contributor, it is still amazing to me, and possibly to you, Ladies, that a woman who does not wear makeup and who *does not color her hair* can be this much in love.

"*Some* men are not completely heinous, I admit," I say. Of

course I'm going to concede it. The fourth Giantess could pick me up with one hand, twirl me around her head, and toss me into the heated serving platters of scrambled eggs. "But the question is," I say, "What Do We *Need* Men For? I'm driving across the country and asking because I have an excellent plan for getting *rid* of men. But first I have to figure out if we *need* them for anything."

"Don't worry," says the first Giantess. "We *don't* need 'em. A woman can work a farm by herself."

And with that, I am dismissed from their magnificent company, and as I am still walking backward, flapping my hand goodbye and exiting the dining room with the plate of scrambled eggs for Lewis, an elegant woman with short dark hair, an umber suede jacket, and makeup so perfect I wonder if Pat McGrath is staying at the Drury Lane Hotel, stops me and says, "Yard work."

"I beg your pardon?" I say.

"That's what we need men for."

But little dare I imagine what smiles and barks of happiness await the waffles as I enter the room.

"500" FESTIVAL ASSOCIATES, INC.
SCHEDULE OF EVENTS FOR ALL 33 GIRLS

You will be honored by the people of your State and Nation during the months of April, May, and June, 1963, in a manner that will both please and surprise you.* We have many terrific events, each of special significance, which you will be attending.

Friday, April 19, 9:00 AM
Indianapolis Athletic Club. Meeting of all candidates with the judges and Queen's Committee. Brunch served. *Dress suggestion: Simple day time dress or suit. No hats or gloves.*

Friday, April 19, 5:00 PM
Indianapolis Athletic Club. Buffet dinner for all candidates and judges. *Dress suggestion: Informal cocktail dress. No hats or gloves.*

Saturday, April 27, 5:30 PM
Indianapolis Athletic Club. Formal dinner. All 33 girls, judges, Queen Committee. *Dress suggestion: All princesses wear short formal gowns.*

---

* I *am* quoting. Exactly. Fifty-six years have passed since I donned that "complete costume." *Today's* 500 Festival honors the most altruistic, ambitious, intellectually driven young women in the state. The Princesses participate in the "500 Festival Leadership Development Program," and visit hospitals and schools. The winner is called the 500 Festival Queen *Scholar*. It is probably the most relevant Queen program in the country.

Wednesday, May 1, 11:15 AM

Indianapolis Motor Speedway Track. Opening Day Ceremony of "500." *Dress suggestion: A complete costume will be furnished to each of the 33 girls and you will be expected to wear this to this event.*

Saturday, May 18, 3:30 PM

Indiana Roof Ballroom. All 33 girls will be brought to the Ballroom from the track under police escort. Your date for the Ball must meet you at the Ballroom at 3:30 PM. *Dress suggestion for escort: Tie and Jacket. Girls, if possible bring a brief description of the formal you will wear for the Ball.*

Saturday, May 25, 6:00 PM

Lincoln-Sheraton Hotel. Dinner with escorts prior to Ball. For all 33 girls. *Dress suggestion: Wear costumes which have been provided to you. Escorts are to come in formal attire. (White dinner jackets.)* **Chaperones:** Mr. & Mrs. Clark, Mr. & Mrs. Huesing, Mr. & Mrs. Kittle.

Saturday, May 25, 7:00 PM

Sheraton Hotel dressing rooms. Change into formals.

Saturday, May 25, 8:15 PM

Leave hotel and cross street to Coronation Ball—Indiana Roof Ballroom.

Tuesday, May 28

"500" Festival Parade. Transportation to the floats from the Marriott Hotel will be provided. All 33 girls will ride in Parade on a float. After Parade you will be taken back to Marriott Hotel where you will change into costume provided.

> **Thursday, May 30 (Time to be announced)**
> Indianapolis Athletic Club. Assemble for trip to Indianapolis Motor
> Speedway and "500" Race. All 33 girls and escorts to attend. *Dress
> suggestion. Wear costumes provided.*

The main "costume provided" is a chic black sheath. The cars
assigned to us, which, oddly, are not mentioned in the schedule,
are Limited Edition Chrysler 300 Pace Setter convertibles. I have
removed the Sunday, May 26, 3:30 P.M service to honor Gold
Star Mothers, the Tuesday, May 28, 10:30 P.M. "Square Dance,"
and the Wednesday, May 29, 9:30 P.M. "Musical Festival," from
the above. Though my memory is like a mastodon caught in a tar
pit, I have absolutely no recollection of these events. What I remember is the "Saturday, May 25, 7:00 P.M. Sheraton Hotel
dressing room."

I remember the Sheraton Hotel dressing room because my
escort, Mike Troy—the Olympic gold medal winner, the famous
cover of *Sports Illustrated,* love of my life, owner of a '57 Ford he
named Rocinante—and I sneak out of the ball and return to the
room to make out, and one of the chaperones, looking for a for-
getful Princess's bracelet, opens the door and surprises us
french-kissing on the bed.

"*What,*" she inquires with a terrific scream, her hand fluttering to her throat, "are you *doing?*"

I can't remember if this chaperone is Mrs. Clark, Mrs. Huesing, or Mrs. Kittle.

"We're working on my English paper!" I say.

"Go back to the dance at once!" she screeches, covering her
eyes with her hand.

"Just looking for Jeanie's *Bell Jar,*" says Mike, who is valiant
and honorable and loves his country and as a young navy lieu-

tenant will ship off to Vietnam with the UDTs (Underwater Demolition Teams later known as the SEALs).*

"I am reporting you" says Mrs. Chaperone in a stricken trill, "to the Queen Committee!"

These are the days when "our boys" can jump out of planes, swim up rivers, lose all four of their limbs, and die for their country but are not allowed to roll around with a girl on a Sheraton Hotel bed. Mrs. Chaperone, bracing herself against a table so she won't collapse, and, clutching her hair and turning her flaming eyes away from us, shivers the other hand toward the open door.

"Out!"

"Good night!" says Mike, seizing her arm on our way out and shaking her hand warmly.

"Out!"

I have been reprimanded once before. A horrible little man on the Queen Committee who thinks that he is orchestrating the wedding of Princess Grace and Prince Rainier of Monaco—the very man who perhaps ignites my devoted lifelong disrespect for the entire sex, and therefore comes in at **#10** on **The Most Hideous Men of My Life List**—censures me for shouting at some cute mechanics from a tower I'd climbed at the racetrack, and so, frankly, Ladies, my prospects for Queenship and giving Parnelli Jones the milk are not looking real good.

---

* I'm not 100 percent sure Mike said *Bell Jar.* It could have been *The Feminine Mystique,* though I doubt it, as Betty Friedan's book didn't become a massive bestseller until four or five months later.

The fierce rush of the Four Giantesses, the free breakfasts at the Drury Inn (not the Drury *Lane,* as I've been calling it), the free dinners, the free wine, the free popcorn, the free hot dogs, and the indoor swimming pool of the Drury Inn are enough to make me forget Miss Bingley, so it is dashing the cup of joy from my lips when Ashley calls from Coad Toyota to say that the estimate is now $2,166 and that Miss Bingley "also" needs a new axle.

"I'll be right over!" I shout.

It requires a strong nervous system and plenty of womanly confidence to speak with a Bingley mechanic. I put on my short velvet jacket and Stewart hunting plaid kilt, and, with Lewis looking like Sir Walter Raleigh in his black collar and ruff of multicolored ribbons, we raise our courage by *jogging* to Coad Toyota.

We are just turning into the entrance of Coad, and I am, of course, passionately occupied with the $2,166 and wondering how I am going to pay it, when a chili-red truck—a Jester!—goes by, and the guy in the passenger seat yells—Ladies, I beg your pardon; the guy *shouts,* "Are you fucking that dog?" Or possibly, "Is that dog fucking you?" And Lewis cuts in front of me to run and kiss them, and I somersault over him and land on my face.

If I didn't have such a thick skull, it would have been the end of your advice columnist. Of course, the left knee is smashed and the right elbow is sprained, and a salesman from Toyota runs out the front doors, exclaiming, "You flew—*flew* into the air! I thought you were dead!"

So this is the story of how **#8**, Danny the Mechanic at Cleopatra Automotive 118 miles away in Blytheville, Arkansas, comes to cause my two black eyes and broken nose:

He abuses Miss Bingley so badly, she loses her brakes in Pocahontas, is assailed by **#9** Stocky Man, is towed to Coad Toyota in Cape Girardeau, where **#11** on **The Most Hideous Men of My Life List** drives by in a chili-red truck and asks if I am fucking my dog (or if my dog is fucking me), and that dog causes me to fly over his back and land on my coconut.

P.S. It will come as no surprise that my Pi Beta Phi sorority sister, the beautiful Kokomo Indiana farm girl Miss Linda Lou Mugg (last seen crowning me on page 71)—whose mother once found a jar of Vaseline in the barn and confronted Linda Lou with it, though Linda Lou had *no idea what she was talking about*—deservingly becomes Queen of the Indy 500 and presents Parnelli Jones with the bottle of milk.

Indianapolis 500 Princesses. If you can find your advice columnist, I will buy you a bottle of milk. Let me know at E.Jean@AskEJean.com. Photo by the illustrious William R. Cale, who photographed more than 1,000 princesses in his day.

VII

"He Will Actually Put His Head Down So Molly and Sally Can Pee on His Face."

Marianna, Arkansas
(#1,078 Most Popular Girl's Name)

Eudora, Arkansas
(#13,325 Most Popular Girl's Name)

WHEN TOURING THE RURAL HAMLETS OF THE SOUTH:

1. Arrive in hamlet.
2. Find place to park near town square.
3. Turn off Miss Bingley.
4. Attach leash to Lewis Carroll.
5. Walk down main street and look at dead guy.
6. Eat in café named after woman.
7. Walk up main street and look at dead guy.
8. Remove leash.
9. Get back in car.
10. Drive.
11. Arrive in new hamlet.
12. Find place to park near town square.
13. Turn off Miss Bingley.
14. Attach leash to Lewis Carroll.
15. Walk down main street and look at dead guy.

The dead guy in Marianna, Arkansas, is on top of a marble column twenty feet high with cannons at the bottom aimed at passersby. Around the dead guy is a little park with benches and a gazebo, and on the edge of the park is a building, a big long thing with an elevated sidewalk and a balustrade, and leaning over the balustrade, opposite the dead guy, is an old African American man watching a white lady of doubtful age in a . . . a—WHAT THE HELL IS THAT? SOME SORT OF IRISH GETUP?— walking some kind of French saltine cracker dog with a New Orleans bowl cut, and the old man stares at the woman as she walks toward him with a look on his face that says, "Lady-I'll-pay-you-forty-dollars-not-to-speak-to-me."

"Why aren't there any statues of women?" I ask him.

He lowers his eyeballs into their pouches.

"You got dead guys on statues *everywhere!*" I cry as Lewis repeatedly tries to leap over the balustrade and kiss the man. "You got a dead guy on top of that column right over there," I say, pointing.

The old man lifts his very fine steamed-and-rolled straw hat and replaces it on the side of his head at such a thoughtful angle, I know I'm about to receive a reply, and I back up a step to give him space to ruminate.

"W-e-e-e-e-e-e-e-el-l-l . . ." he says.

[Long pause.]

I am learning not to rush conversations in the South.

[Long pause.]

"Sin women," he says, pronouncing the words *sin women* with about thirty syllables, and takes another long pause.

"Sin women . . . ?" I say.

"Sin womens *raaaaiiiiizzzzzed* [eighteen syllables] money to build that statue, why you askin' *meeeee* why there ain't no statues of women?"

"Wait. *What!?*"

I turn around and look at the thing.

"*Women* raised the money to build that? What women?"

The old man says:

"D——————————————————— ——————————

————————————————————————."

I can't possibly connect all two or three hundred syllables contained in his answer—a veritable concerto of musical notes—

quickly enough to understand immediately that he's saying, "Daughters of the Confederacy," but when I do, I am, of course, twice as disgusted.

"They's the ones," he says.

By the way, Ladies, the marble column with the dead guy on top is carved on all four sides with poetry so fine it sounds like dialogue from *The Walking Dead*.

> *Dead heroes! Did we*
> *hear one say?*
> *Dead, never! They will*
> *live for aye* . . . . . .

"But *men* are the morons who start wars and get shot!" I say. And just when I'm about to add the obvious conclusion, "*So why do women have to pay for it,*" I notice what the dead guy is wearing.

"Oh my God!" I cry. "His boots!"

The old man squints at the statue.

"Correct me if I'm wrong, sir," I say, "but I believe those are Chanel over-the-knees from 2016!!"

This makes the old man chuckle, and he lifts the hat and puts the hat back on the side of his head. Swear to God, that hat could have its own Instagram.

"So how come women have to pay for some dead guy* wearing Chanel boots?" I say.

"Well . . . " says the old man, "men's the *boss.*"

---

* I looked up the statue later, and it turned out to be the famous nincompoop Robert E. Lee. Had I known at the time it was the commander of the Confederacy States Army, a man who believed neither women nor blacks should have the vote, no doubt the old man and I would have had a very different conversation, and he would have asked me to accompany him to the Twin Hogs Bar-B-Que for a snack, and I would have invited him to visit me in New York, and we would have gone to see *Hamilton*, and so on. But, incredibly, I didn't think to ask, "*Who's* the dead guy?"

I will tell you about my boss, Ladies; *my* boss happens to be an organized crime boss, but first, just let me stick my head in— won't take a moment—we happen to be passing Hightower and Sons Funeral Home, Ladies, and, "If *anyone* is an expert on dead men," I say, opening the door and addressing a tall, gorgeous African American man dressed in the Wall Street banker mode, gray- and white-striped shirt with white collar, light gray Brooks Brothers trousers, "it must be you."

"I will answer any question you have," says the courtly Mr. Hightower, who has served on the Marianna City Counsel for thirty-four years.

"Who lives happier lives in Marianna?" I say. "Men or women?"

"Fifty-fifty," says Mr. Hightower.

"Who is mourned more in Marianna when they die? Men or women?"

"Women," says Mr. Hightower.

"Who weeps more when a loved one dies in Marianna? Men or women?"

"Women."

"Who causes more deaths in Marianna? Men or women?"

"Men."

"Who has a bunch of statues built to remember them? Men or women?"

"Men."

"Who lives longer in Marianna? Men or women?"

"Women."

I rest my case.

Lewis and I can now go to lunch, and I can tell you about my boss, The Neck.

I meet The Neck at Gino's East restaurant in Chicago, where I am hostess.

Never has your advice columnist's lack of all talent been put to better advantage than as greeter-and-seater at Gino's! I shimmer back and forth between the booths in my see-through crocheted minidress, my Running Naked body stocking, my two-toned vanilla cream and banana bisque shoes with stacked heels, and eat on a daily basis—I am not exaggerating—fourteen or fifteen slices of pizza, plus two baskets of Italian bread, plus another basket of garlic bread, plus twenty or thirty pats of butter, plus four, five, six scoops of spumoni. Ladies, you just have no conception how delicious and famous Gino's East pizza is in 1968—it is, in fact, *the* Chicago pizza. TV glamorosi, local political illuminati, journalists, gawkers, stalkers, and mob guys drop by the basement spot on Superior Street, just off glittering Michigan Avenue.

I am new in the hostessing racket, but already I am developing my "hostess style," and my hostess style is to sit up front in the restaurant, which is long, dark, and cavernous, like the pens under the Roman Colosseum, where Caligula kept his juiciest Christians—it is my style, I say, to have a dish of ice cream always in front of me, and I am cramming in about fifteen dollars' worth of spumoni when **#12** on **The Most Hideous Men of My Life List** appears in the doorway. The bartender bats me the high sign (i.e., the alarmed look of someone who's just seen a horse head among the Chianti bottles), and I jump up in my see-through crocheted mini and greet The Neck.*

To The Neck's right, as he enters Gino's East, is the bar with the frightened bartender, who is having a secret affair with the black-haired waitress, who is actually a natural blonde.

To The Neck's left is the big table. The big table is where the Italian Mafia sit. These guys *never* sit in back. The back is darker than the Vatican catacombs. The back is darker than a child abuser's black cassock.

I greet The Neck.

The Neck hands me a twenty-dollar bill.

"Oh!" I shout. "Gosh!"

I hand it back to him and gesture to the big table, which is about seven steps inside the door.

The Neck puts the twenty back into my hand.

"For you."

"Ohhhhh! Heavens!" I say.

---

* Ladies, I do not know a thing about organized crime—except that it is composed of male lunatics—but I think even the Federal Bureau of Investigation would agree that the Chicago mob reached its absolute peak of glamour during the period I am trying to write about here, with Giancana and Battaglia, neither of whom I'd ever heard of at the time, being a farm girl from Indiana. Al Capone in Chicago and John Dillinger, a handsome Indiana boy who got himself shot in front of Chicago's Biograph Theater, was about the extent of my mob knowledge.

I put the twenty on the table where I have commanded The Neck to sit.

"You're new?" says The Neck coyly. "You're taking over for Margie?"* As he speaks, The Neck slides the twenty off the table and tries to put it in my hand again. I clasp both my hands behind my back, laugh, turn, and sit down at my spumoni.

The next day, at the same time—early, 5:30 or so in the afternoon—The Neck appears in the doorway.

Dressed like a million dollars, fat as a clam, big as a whale with a head larger than an ice chest, and a neck like a highway girder, he grins shyly past the bartender at me.

I drop my spoon. I leap to my feet. I shimmer over to greet him.

The Neck puts a fifty in my hand.

"Ohhhhhhhhhhhhhh!" I say, and I give it back to him.

"I want you to have it," says The Neck.

"Sit!" I say, laughing, stepping to the big table and pulling out his chair. "SIT!!"

The bartender almost passes out in fright.

This time, when The Neck leaves, after drinking a half cup of coffee, he walks over and slyly places the fifty on my table next to my spumoni, and I roll it in a ball and throw it at him as he steps out the door. I get him in the ear.

The next day, The Neck doesn't show. Nor the next. The bartender spends every spare minute telling me about The Neck, and The Neck, according to the bartender, is an "underboss," and, as P. G. Wodehouse says, if not definitely Public Enemy Number One, then absolutely number twelve or thirteen, and by the way, *The Neck* is my name for him.†

---

* Margie! Hello, wherever you are, you paragon of womanhood! I remember the night one of my friends took a photo of you. You were wearing your trim gray suit cut like Kim Novak's in *Vertigo*, and you made my friend open his camera, remove the entire roll of film, and hand it to you!

† Incredibly, though, I've kept a daily diary since I was nine, and I yak about The Neck

The next two days I have off. When I return, The Neck appears in the doorway.

I push away my spumoni, stand, and shimmer over.

He puts a hundred-dollar bill in my hand.

I return it.

He gives it back.

I return it.

He gives it back.

I return it.

"I think he has a crush on you," says Sam, the owner of Gino's, the next day. "He doesn't eat. He doesn't drink. He doesn't order. You got a boyfriend, Jeanie." In the middle of this conversation, The Neck appears in the doorway.

The Neck slams Sam on the back. Sam shakes The Neck's hand. The waitress who is having the affair with the bartender brings two coffees, and The Neck and Sam sit down at the big table and goggle at me.

My God, I am fantastic!

My eyes look like billiard balls that have rolled accidentally into a bucket of black paint, so slathered are my lids in the Twiggy style—false-eyelashed to the gills, eyelined, shadowed, with lower lashes *drawn* on. My hair is parted in the middle, pulled back into a low ponytail, like the Marquis de Sade, and tied with a pale grosgrain ribbon into a bow.

And my frock? My frock will knock you out! A short floaty thing of sheer Show-It-All Alabaster curtain material that I sewed. I wear it over the Running Naked body stocking.

And, Ladies, let me tell you that old body stocking is getting quite a workout, because I am, within a week, the best hostess in the history of pizza-joint hostessing, greeting everyone with a "Wow! Hello! Hello! Hello!" and then whirling around and tear-

---

in my Chicago diaries— "his cufflinks are as big as pie pans," etc., etc. I never mention him by name! My internet searches have not turned him up—yet.

ing down the restaurant like a reconnaissance jet on a runway, calculating which waitresses have which tables, and just before reaching the booth I have decided upon, twirling myself into a slide so my floaty dress wafts out, skidding to a halt, cocking my head at the assigned booth, and (if it is a Friday or Saturday night), pulling slow eaters *out* of their booths or piling perfect strangers together *into* booths, and taking food off customers' plates and eating it. Nobody has seen smoke like this since Mrs. Whats-Her-Name's cow started the Chicago fire!

Sam motions me over to where he is sitting with The Neck at the big table and tells me that The Neck has "something to ask" me. Having performed the preliminary sweetening up, Sam leaves, saying, in an enthusiastic whisper, to The Neck:

"Go ahead."

The Neck appears nervous. He looks down at the table like he's just shot somebody by mistake.

"Would you like to go to dinner?" he says.

"Love to!" I say. "But I don't get off work till after 2:00 A.M."

"I mean," says The Neck, humbly dropping one of his chins, "next Monday. Sam says you have Monday off."

"Oh, dear. My parents will be in town for a visit!" I say with disarming mendacity.

The next three times The Neck asks me to dinner, I am "babysitting for my friend," "volunteering at the nursing home," and "taking a night class."

"Jeanie, your admirer has a proposal for you," says Sam one day to me not long after the "night class" rejection.

"Oh! I like proposals!" I say.

"Can you come early tomorrow?" says Sam. "You'll have some privacy."

"Sit down," says The Neck when I appear early the next day in my see-through crocheted mini, body stocking, stacked heels, hair pulled back in a bow, and eyes lacquered till they look like sandwich plates singed in a campfire.

I perch at the end of a chair at "our table."

The Neck looks at my forehead with a frightened smile, like he just found out Eliot Ness has been discovered alive in the Chicago River.

"I have a proposal," he says.

"Did you bring a ring?" I say.

There are no cowards in hostessing.

"Something better," says The Neck, whose neck looks twice as large as usual, and he swells it out and heaves a romantic sigh. We are alone. The bartender hasn't shown up yet.

Beholding The Neck close up, his yellowish ice-chest face, his tufts of brown hair, his dark eyes trapped inside his cheeks, Ferrante & Teicher playing in the background (Sam!!), is almost more than I can take. *Heavens to Murgatroyd!* I'm thinking. *I hope he doesn't get down on one knee!*

"Are you Catholic?" says The Neck.

"I was raised Catholic," I say.

"We have a lot in common," says The Neck.

I can see he is working up to something, trying to marshal his charm.

"It's a nice day," he says.

"Wonderful," I say.

Perhaps if he just pulled his gun, it would move things along.

"I would like to buy you the car of your choice," he says.

"I'll take a white Corvette," I say.

"Plus, I am offering you $1,000 a week, plus $5,000 for clothes, your apartment paid for, and all expenses."

Ladies, let me translate those 1968 numbers into roughly current sums for you:

"Plus, I am offering you $7,272.09 a week, plus $36,360.47 for clothes, your apartment paid for, and all expenses."

"Heavens to Betsy!" I cry.

He unloads another sigh and looks into my eyes.

"Think it over," he says.

He places his hand over mine.

The code of the Cosa Nostra, I suppose, prevents him from ravishing me on the spot.

"Oh! I will! No one has ever asked me to be a mistress before!"

And with that, he stands, and, buttoning his dark cashmere coat, which he never took off, and, dropping two last amorous nods of his chins, exits Gino's East, climbs the stairs to the street, his driver opens the door of his big black Lincoln, which seems as long as a yacht, and he rolls away. And to this day, I don't know whether he is shot, drowns in a cement suit in Lake Michigan, leaves the country, dies of apoplexy, or is arrested by the cops, but none of us sees hide nor hair of The Neck again.

7 ⋯⋯⋯⋯▶

"Who lies to cops more? Men or women?"

"Everybody lies."

"But who lies more?" I say.

I am asking Officer Acosta of the Marianna Police Department. He is lunching in Subway. His partner, Officer Harris, a courtly woman who freezes a teenager against his own Ford pickup in the parking lot with a look, is also at the table. They are dining on six-inch footlongs.

I have tailed the officers from the Hightower and Sons Funeral Home, through Marianna, and into Subway, where I have ordered my usual—the CEO of Subway being a woman, Subway has received the What Do We Need Men For Stamp of Approval—two nine-grain footlongs, toasted, with cheddar, Monterey Jack, and swiss cheese, spinach, tomatoes, green peppers, carrots, red onions, olives, and several ladlefuls of mustard, and have accosted Officer Acosta.

"Men or women—who lies more?"

"Men," says Officer Acosta.

"Women lie more when they want to get charges dropped on the men they *brought* charges against," says Officer Harris.

"So, both of you must be pretty good at lie-detecting?" I say.

"Yes."

"Then it must be difficult for your lovers to win arguments with you," I say.

"My wife's a cop too," says Officer Acosta. *"Nobody* wins an argument."

And just as the conversation is turning interesting, a call comes in, and both officers hurriedly wad up their napkins, and, as Officer Acosta wipes their table with his sandwich wrapper, he says to me with pleasure fizzing in his eyes, "It never stops!"

Ladies! What's your latest project? When was the last time you drove to Home Depot, debouched from your car, and gaggled toward the door, poking people in the eye with the old yardstick you brought along to help to pick out and measure the fourteen lengths of five-inch crown molding?

My last time is 215 miles ago at Lowe's, when I run into farmer Linda McFarland. We meet in the parking lot, where an excited woman tightly wrapped in a white trench coat climbs out of her Jeep Wrangler, gallops into the entrance, gallops out a moment later, retrieves *her* piece of old measuring stick from the Jeep, and gallops back into the store while a golden retriever in a Land Rover next to the Jeep* sits gazing and howling at Lewis from behind his half-rolled-up window.

"What's your project, Miss Linda?"

"I'm putting up some pictures."

"You need to go buy a hammer?"

"Oh, I *got* my hammers, my drills," says Linda, whose blond hair looks like it was cut by the same person who did Demi Moore's in *G.I. Jane.* "I got my own tools, my own shop full of

---

*Where the *hell* all these women are going in all these big four-wheel-drive vehicles when it is flat as a pancake around here beats me!

tools, so anything that breaks, I fix it. I don't [*Whomp!* A smile explodes on her face.] need a man to do it. No! I have a friend who's been supporting a man for fifteen years, and he hasn't worked *a day!*"

"The loafer!" I cry.

"Now, if I could find a *real* man," says Miss Linda, "one that knew how to work, but all I have to do is mention that I have a 120-acre farm, and the men *ruuuuuuuuuuuuunnnnnnnnnnnn*. It's the cattle that gets them. I got some Black Angus, and then I got some Red Angus, and I got one that looks like she's gonna pop, but she ain't popped yet, so I have to keep an eye 'cause last year I had a cow deliver her calf right on the top of a big steep hill, and that calf came out and slid all the way down that hill to the *bottom* of the pasture, and I just knew he would be hurt, broken leg, a little red bull calf. But he was fine!"

"Whew!" I say.

"And I got my goats, Sally, Molly, and Willy. Willy is the boyfriend. He will actually put his head down so Molly and Sally can pee on his face. I don't know if he thinks it attracts those girls or not! And I got the rabbits, Wilma, Betty, and Fred, and nine new babies! And I got my chickens, I sell my organic eggs in town, I got giant Brahmas, gray and black, and the males are curly and they're about THIS big."

She holds out her arms to indicate a chicken as big as a basset hound.

"And then I have Lavenders, which is another gray, a real pale gray, and they have a white circle on their ear that looks almost like an earring. Very pretty. I also have Barred Rocks; they're striped. Gray and black. And I have an Araucana that lays green eggs, and sometimes blue! And her name is Gypsy, and her mate is Jackson."

Ladies, never in your life have you seen such grinning, beaming, exploding, cracking, and smiling as the Chicken Lady of Lowe's standing here in the parking lot talking about her birds.

"And then the Barred Rocks have their own rooster; his name is Knight. He has two hens, Curly and Princess."

After each breed report, Linda whomps a smile on her map as big as anything, making her rose-tinted glasses, which are shaped like seagull wings, fly up and down on her nose.

"Knight takes care of Curly and Princess in a studly fashion, and he also takes care of Gypsy, the Araucana, in a studly fashion, though he isn't supposed to. Though he does. And so now when I get ready to hatch their eggs, I'll separate them for thirty days to make sure the chicks are full blood. But for *taste?* My Cinnamon Queens' eggs taste the best. They lay a lot of double-yolkers. Oh my God! If you ever eat an organic Cinnamon Queen egg, you'll never eat another regular egg in your life! And my roosters? They just strut. And when they want to have sex, they just jump on the hen and *do it.*"

"Sounds like Harvey Weinstein," I say.

Linda looks at me. "Who?"

"Harvey Weinstein? You know Harvey Weinstein, the Hollywood producer?"

"No."

"He's the accused 1,300-pound serial rapist who flies around the world banging on hotel room doors and brutalizing talented women."

"Oh."

And her smile slowly, slowly, slowly disappears.*

What have I done? I am so stupid! Here is the happiest woman on earth, never met a chicken she didn't like, rocks her little hen, Gypsy, to sleep in her arms at night, and I drag Weinstein, the giant bloodsucking tick, across the Lowe's parking lot? What the hell's the matter with me? Better change the subject.

---

* Miss Linda is not the only person I meet whose smile I wipe off with Weinstein. The incredible fact is, outside of New York, *many* people—at the time the What Do We Need Men For trip is happening—have not heard of Weinstein.

"Why don't lady farmers color their hair?" I say.

Boom!

Up go the rose-tinted glasses!

"In New York," I say, "we start hitting the hair color at thirty-five, thirty-six. I can see you're a natural blonde, Miss Linda; but what's going on with farm women? Is it against the law to dye your hair?"

"Well, to be truthful," says Linda, "it costs a lot of money to go to the beauty shop and have it colored. And also the men."

"What about the men?" I say.

"The men say, 'I don't care what your hair looks like, just cook my supper.'"

"In New York," I say, "ninety-seven-year-old dames have hair the shade of baby chicks and still try to please men."

"I've never been to New York!" says Linda. "But I'd love to go!"

"You and your roosters would be a big hit there!" I say.

"Oh, I tell ya!" says Linda. "On Saturdays when I go to Fruitland for the farm swap, I load 'em all up, my chickens, my rabbits, maybe a couple of goats in the back of my Ford truck, and if I don't swap or sell them, I got 'em in the back of the truck, and I'm coming back home, and I'm stopping at yard sales in town with the chickens in the back going *auahak! auahak! auahak!* People *love* to see me comin'!"

Linda is the Beyoncé of agriculture.

"What Do We Need Men For?" I say.

"Nuthin'," says Linda. "At least I don't."

"Who do you think would run America better? Men or women?"

"We're friendlier," says Linda, "have more common sense, and if someone attacked our children, we'd fight. Women would be better."

"So if we get rid of the men for a couple of years while we run things, where do you suggest we put them?"

"We should put them somewhere they'd learn to treat women better."

"Can we put them on your farm for a couple of years?"

"Yes!" says Linda, fishing into her quilted Vera Bradley bag and handing me her card. "But *I'm the boss.* They'd have to do what I tell them!"

"OK, gentlemen!" I say to the crème of alpha male society, the six Men of Marianna who meet at Subway for lunch. "Whattya think of putting all the men in America on a farm, and letting a *woman* be the boss and run the country for a while?"

The men consider for a moment.

"Depends on what she looks like," says Mr. Tommy Triplett.

Now, Ladies, what we have here are the illuminati of the manly sex: a rancher (Mr. Keith Cranford), a farmer and All-American football player (Mr. Bill Curtis), a chap who has had three wives (Mr. Phillip McClurg), a big-deal retired military officer (Mr. Jim Cox), another rich farmer (Mr. Rusty Carter), and a retired flower and tree nursery magnate (Mr. Triplett) who was voted Most Beautiful Baby in the Tri-States—Mississippi, Tennessee, and Arkansas.*

"Are you Irish?" says Mr. Carter. "What's with that getup?"

I try a different angle:

---

* "I thought I had won," says Mr. Triplett. "And everybody in town thought I'd won, but when my mother passed away, I was going through the records, and I discovered I only got *Honorable Mention.*"

"Do you think we'd be fighting constant wars and putting up statues of dead guys if women ran things?"

"Women have too much compassion to start a war," says Mr. Triplett, the beautiful baby.

The Men of Marianna: Phillip McClurg, Keith Cranford, Tommy Triplett, Rusty Carter, Jim Cox, Bill Curtis.

The All-American, Mr. Curtis, a handsome fellow in a green baseball hat, glasses without frames, long cheeks, and ears like Lorna Doone cookies, says, "Women are too immature. They're too wimpy. They're supposed to stay at home and raise a family."

The lads are sitting back, their legs spread to the absolute maximum man-spreading length. I wait for someone to start chuckling, but hold on, Ladies. *Not a peep.* Mr. Curtis, All-American, is dead serious.

"You don't think," I say, smiling, "we'd be better off if women ran things just for a while?"

"Women are not strong enough, physically or mentally, to take care of business," says the All-American.

Ladies, isn't it refreshing to hear a man speak so frankly? In fact, to repay Mr. Curtis for his candor, I think I should go get Carla.

Carla is Cherokee. Cherokee women, as you know, were controlling their own property, approving tribal leaders, marrying and divorcing male nincompoops *at will* for hundreds of years before European women were "allowed" to own a single lace of their own personal corsets. And what does Carla do if a man insults her? Carla *clocks* the chump—oh, *yes!*—knocks him *flat.*

I'll go get Carla, shall I? The lid is off, right? Other women can blog and tweet about #MeToo, which is good; but Carla just *blams* the scoundrels. Carla doesn't talk about it, of *course.* No woman in the secret club talks about it. It is too awesome. Too perfect. They don't want it known. Let "nice" women "build better communication" with the male patriarchy—not Carla, not the members of the secret club. I haven't met them individually, but I receive letters. A whole new life is out there—and when I run into Carla in Eudora ("Catfish Capital of Arkansas"), her little "I'm just a country girl," and her twinkling laughing eyes, and her demure attitude that seems to say, "I don't want to tarnish the luster of immortal woman"—Ladies, I guess she's in the secret club in about three minutes.

If a man acts up, shoves her, corners her, grabs her, she "picks up whatever I can pick up."

"What do you pick up?" I ask.

"With *Carla?*" says her brother, Henry. "A knife."

"Do you ever start the fight?" I ask her.

"No. No," she says.

Carla is a buxom, graceful woman with a powerful frame, a bit of weight, and a gorgeous head of fabulous dark hair pulled into a knot, and I think I should go and fetch her. I'll bring her back to this Marianna Subway, buy a round of Coca-Colas for everybody, introduce the Crème of Marianna Men to her, and let her stand here, cock her hip, and have a word with these good ol' boys.

And while I'm at it, Ladies, every sorority has its insignia, right? Don't we need a secret badge for women who are members of the Carla Club—The Women Who Fight Back—physically or otherwise? What insignia do you suggest? Any ideas? What do you think about one small Band-Aid worn around the finger that is next to the little finger on the left hand?

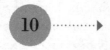

MY BOSSES (SO FAR . . . . . .)

1. **Age:** 11–17. **Job:** Babysitting. **Boss:** Various Fort Wayne mothers and fathers.
2. **Age:** 12–75. **Job:** Filling the US mail with magazine pitches.* **Boss:** Various editors who reject me.
3. **Age:** 18–19. **Job:** Governessing. **Boss:** Mr. and Mrs. Robert Smyth of Chicago and Lake Geneva.
4. **Age:** 19–20. **Job:** Lifeguarding. **Boss:** Supervisor of Fort Wayne outdoor pools.
5. **Age:** 19–20. **Job:** Starting a chain letter. **Boss:** The US Postal Service.†

---

* My first pitch, at age twelve, is to the Sears & Roebuck catalog.

† My dad—the wit of Fort Wayne, the inventor of TV goggles, elongated beds, and

6. **Age:** 20. **Job:** Making amusing hats and selling them on campus. **Boss and Creator:** Myself.

7. **Age:** 21. **Job:** Founding a cheerleading camp. **Boss and Creator:** Myself. (If you can't find a job, *create* a job.)

8. **Age:** 22–23. **Job:** Market researching for Procter & Gamble. **Boss:** VP of research.

9. **Age:** 23–24. **Job:** Creating publicity for Delswa, the largest fashion house in South Africa. **Boss:** Wonderful chap with a very handsome son. I can't recall their names and leave my diary behind.*

10. **Age:** 25. **Job:** Account executing. **Boss:** We're getting to him in a moment.

11. **Age:** 25. **Job:** Hostessing at Gino's East. **Boss:** Sam Levine.

12. **Age:** 29. **Job:** Teaching English and gym at Idaho State Reform School—a place believed to be haunted and investigated on an episode of *Ghost Adventures*. **Boss:** Can't remember his name. The poor man loses his mind when I drive the "juvenile delinquents" over the state line to visit a carnival in a school bus that has no brakes.

13. **Age:** 30. In the face of a spectacular blizzard of rejections from editors, producers, etc., I go on sending out article ideas, stories, plays, quizzes, screenplays, etc., etc., etc.

14. **Age:** 37. **Job:** Writer! Miss Marilyn Johnson (hi, Marilyn!), editor at *Esquire,* snatches off the slush pile—*by chance*—something I send in. She buys it, and I get my

---

sugar-coated cereal—starts, in Fort Wayne, a whiskey chain letter (you send the person at the top of your list a bottle of whiskey), which gives me the idea of starting a chain letter at Indiana University—not with whiskey. With money. With the school swearing to discipline the "ringleaders," I escape detection and make about $2,100.

* I tramp around Africa after P&G, bop down to see Kruger National Park in South Africa, end up taking a job in Johannesburg—this is years before Nelson Mandela ends Apartheid—get to know some Zulu "agitators," hold a few meetings in my apartment, and leave the diary behind when I am "asked" by the dreaded CID (criminal investigation division) to leave South Africa in something of a flurry.

size 11 shoe in the door, and when the door at *Esquire*
opens, I squeeze into *Outside, Playboy, Rolling Stone, New
York, Glamour,* etc.

15. **Age:** 43. **Job:** Writing for *Saturday Night Live.* **Boss:**
    Lorne Michaels.
16. **Age:** 50. **Job:** Writing the Ask E. Jean column in *Elle.*
    Boss: Four editors in chief have reigned during my tenure:
    Amy Gross hired me, Elaina Richardson put up with me,
    Robbie Myers delighted me, and Nina Garcia inspires me.
17. **Age:** 51. **Job:** Hosting the *Ask E. Jean* TV show. **Boss:**
    Roger Ailes, soon to be making an appearance.
18. **Age:** 69. **Job:** Founding Tawkify Inc. **Bosses and
    Creators:** Myself and Kenneth Shaw.
19. **Age:** 75. **Job:** Writing this St. Martin's book you are
    holding in your beautifully manicured grip, Ladies. **Boss:**
    It is edited by the sensational Elisabeth Dyssegaard.

Damn! Look at it! Is that Procter & Gamble at #8? Is that the
most fabulous job a girl could ever have? Does P&G send me all
over this marvelous country to talk to housewives about their
toilet paper, shampoo, toothpaste, laundry detergent, room fresh-
ener, and, most memorably, a new sanitary napkin that is shaped
like a headband and which I personally "place" with practically
every demographically menstruating woman between the ages of
eighteen and forty-four in Atlanta, Georgia? Procter & Gamble
is the only "real" job I ever have.

Smashingly dressed, and making $520 a week, I, a P&G market
researcher, fly into a city, rent a car, drive to the neighborhood cho-
sen by the demographic scientists back in Cincinnati, exit the car,
walk up to the first house, knock on the door, the "lady of the house"
opens the door—repeat, *opens the door!* (i.e., she is *at home*)—and after
introducing myself, *I am invited in!* In the *house.* This is a mere fifty
years ago. Today, this seems almost more incredible than the fact that
my mother lets me walk to the store alone at four years old.

I learn to strike up conversations with *anyone*. The key: I am just waaaaaaay more interested in the person than in myself.

I suppose I should also mention that from #11 to #14, I marry and live ecstatically on a ranch in Ennis, Montana, where my husband is a logger and forest firefighter. He fly-fishes. I spend my days on my horse, Miss Hot, a bay (!) quarter horse with the disposition of Lady Macbeth. I spend evenings in "the shed," an old pump house, working through the night eating grapefruits and writing the magazine articles, quizzes, stories, novels, movie scripts, etc., etc., which no one buys. Not long after Marilyn Johnson, at *Esquire,* plucks me out of oblivion, *Outside* sends me to New York to take Fran Lebowitz camping, and I like the Big City so much, I *stay.*

Prairie dresses! My sister Barbie Carroll is flower girl, Nancy Gift and Nancy Logan (née Kesler) are both maids of honor, and Steve Byers is my husband. Nancy Logan, the former Miss Chicago, and I remain best friends to this very hour. Steve goes on to become editor in chief of *Outdoor Life.*

And there listed at #18 is old Tawkify. Kenneth is twenty-three and just out of Stanford, and I am an ambitious young twat of sixty-eight, when we start this little company together. And now we have 185 employees, and it's the largest matchmaking company in the country. Kenneth is CEO and running it fantastically. Wait. WHAT AM I TALKING ABOUT?

This is a book *without* good guys.

Forget Kenneth.

All right. Here's Kenneth. Now erase him from your minds, Ladies. We are about to meet **#13** on **The Most Hideous Men of My Life List.**

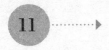

After Johannesburg, I arrive in Chicago and meet one of those semi-good-looking, brown-haired, unimpeachably-but-forgettably -dressed young men who is a vice president because his father owns the company, and the company he is vice president of is an employment agency and accounting firm–type thing, which, despite the gloss of its golden promise, no longer exists.

He hires me to help "land new accounts."

"You start tonight," he says.

"Great!" I say.

"We're meeting the people from Marshall Field's. Be at the Pump Room at eight o'clock."

"Wow!" I say. "The Pump Room!"*

---

* The Pump Room was in the Ambassador East Hotel. John Steinbeck stayed at the Ambassador East in *Travels with Charley*. Alfred Hitchcock shot some of *North by Northwest* there, and they say Bacall and Bogart celebrated their marriage in Booth One of the Pump Room, etc., etc. It was one of the greatest hotels and restaurants in the world.

Congo-green paisley taffeta dinner suit, whisk-broom eyelashes, Rorschach-inkblot eye shadow, stacked heels, Marquis de Sade hair bow, Romping in the Tulips body stocking, and skirt *up to here,* I arrive in the Pump Room. I remember lots of white linen. Lots and lots and lots of white linen. Flowers. Sparkling silver.

The maître d' escorts me to a booth, not Booth One, where Natalie Wood and Robert Wagner canoodled, but a *very* good booth on the right side of the room, where **#13** on **The Most Hideous Men of My Life List** rises to greet me and says:

"They canceled."

"Oh, dear," I say.

"Never mind," he says. "Sit down."

He orders drinks, an extra glass of ice, tells me in detail about the new suit he is wearing, and then says, surprised, "Oh, damn! My ex-wife just walked in."

I spring the false eyelashes open like parasols.

A smashingly put-together woman with a flamboyant mane of rich red hair is being escorted with an older chap (he is probably all of thirty-five) by the maître d' to a table directly across the room. When they are seated, my boss raises his glass to her. She nods and raises one eyebrow at him.

"She's a cunt," he says.

Ten minutes later, an odd thing happens. My boss's ex-wife takes her chap's hand and raises it to her lips. A moment later, my boss takes *my* hand and raises it to his lips.

I jerk my hand away.

"Just a welcome smooch," he says. "Don't be bourgeois."

He pronounces it *booooooozzzzshwhaaa!* and orders another drink. I finish the bread and butter and ask for more. Across the room, my boss's ex-wife glances at us, leans into her chap, and puts her two very, *very* red open lips on her chap's cheek and— well, there is no verb available—*squishes* her lips up and down and sorta rolls them around his face like she is the press-and-steam girl at a dry cleaner. Never seen anything like it before or since.

My boss waits until she concludes. Then he picks up the glass filled with ice, globs in a mouthful, crunches it for about eight seconds, and then plants his freezing lips and tongue on my face.

I nearly fly out of the booth.

"GET OFF!" I cry. "Ewwwwwww!"

"You're *soooo* boooooooozzzzshwahhhhh," says my boss, glob-bing in another mouthful of ice.

"Keep it in your mouth, mister!" I say. "Where's the waiter? I need more bread and butter!"

I am not a foodie, Ladies, as you know. Give me a three-cheese footlong with a mound of red onions on it or a couple of Amy's organic black bean burritos, and I'm happy. But young Jeanie Carroll, The Greenest Employee of the Twentieth Cen-tury, is not about to pass up a dinner in the goddamn Pump Room, I can tell you!

I have filet mignon.*

My boss? I don't recall what he eats, but he orders another drink and becomes more and more excited, telling me I'm *soooo* boooooozzzzshwahhhhhhhhhhh, slobbering on my hand like a Doberman playing with his squeaky toy, and it is probably at about this point when I make a mental note to go to Gino's the

---

* What happened *following* the filet mignon may be one of the reasons I shortly afterward become a vegetarian (and have remained a vegetarian my entire life, so disgusting was this night).

next day and try to get a new job, that my boss's ex-wife, whom I now—fifty years later—suspect is not his ex-wife, but, indeed, his wife, and this is a little game they play to spice things up, starts rubbing her chap's leg.

My boss and I can't actually *see* that she is rubbing her chap's leg, as the table linen hangs nearly to the floor, but it is clear from the feverish action of her shoulders and upper body that she is rubbing and rubbing and rubbing and when her chap's eyes close, she goes on rubbing and rubbing till, in quite a hurry, with his face still smeared with lipstick and looking like a sophomore standing on the free-throw line in a tied game, the chap stands up, heaves a wad of cash on the table, grabs the wife, and they scamper toward the exit.

My boss asks for the check.

My Jean Rhys *Good Morning, Midnight* room in the Eastgate Hotel* on Ontario Street is only a few blocks from the Ambassador East on North State Parkway, but my boss insists on driving me home. It is my first ride in a Mercedes. I am surprised at how really uncomfortable the stiff leather seats are and rank it at no higher than a Jester. Two blocks from my place, my boss runs a red light, stomps the brakes, skids to a halt in the middle of the intersection, and, jabbering about "that cunt" or "a cunt" or "all cunts," jams his hand up and between my legs so hard, I bang my head into the dashboard trying to protect myself.

I open the car door and bolt.

My boss must be doing the following things: driving on through the intersection, stopping, getting out, etc., because as I am about to turn into the Eastgate Hotel, I look back and see him a half block away weaving toward me in a drunken trot. I remember that his legs look menacingly short. I run into the empty hotel lobby. Spurt past the desk. No attendant in sight. Past the elevators. Take the stairs two at a time. Hit the second

---

* It no longer exists, alas.

floor. Feeling for the room key in my jacket pocket, I run down the hall, and, as I put the key in the door, my boss catches me from behind and clamps his teeth on the nape of my neck. I kick backward at his shins, manage to get the key to work, open the door, jab a backward elbow into his ribs, causing a button to fly off my jacket, squeeze into my room and push, push, push, push, push, push the door closed.

Have you ever shut a dog outside who wants to come in, Ladies? My boss scratches and whimpers at that door for the next quarter of an hour.

VIII

"I'm Gonna Run for Mayor!"

Tallulah, Louisiana
(#1,510 Most Popular Girl's Name)

Pearl, Mississippi
(#798 Most Popular Girl's Name)

Verona, Mississippi
(#3,974 Most Popular Girl's Name)

The What Do We Need Men
For Traveling Expenses (So Far . . .)

Ladies, we are about to visit the Hermione Museum in Tallulah, Louisiana, which houses the Madam C. J. Walker exhibit. Madam C. J. Walker is the first female self-made millionaire in America,[*] so it is fitting that we take a look at how much money our What Do We Need Men For road trip is costing.

GAS. . . . . .Well, *Damn!*

I forget to look at the odometer when Lewis and I ooze into Tallulah. Miss Bingley gets an average of fifty miles per gallon. Gas costs \$2.10–\$3.00 a gallon. So let's call it \$2.50 per gallon. We've come—I'm guessing—about two thousand miles. That's forty gallons. So we've spent, as of today, a hundred bucks.

HOTELS. . . . .\$123.26-a-night average

I pay \$95.78 for the Tallulah Super 8 (\$10 more than the latest

---

[*] "I am a woman who came from the cotton fields of the South. From there I was promoted to the washtub. From there I was promoted to the cook kitchen. And from there I promoted myself into the business of manufacturing hair goods and preparations. . . . I have built my own factory on my own ground."—Madam C. J. Walker

reviewer*). Add in pet fees, taxes, late check-out penalties, and tips to the housekeepers. When I give the Tallulah Super 8 housekeeper—a thin, short-haired, overworked woman of sixty or so—a $10 bill, she stares at it in disbelief for a moment and then throws her arms around me. She would probably have fainted dead away if The Neck arrived and handed her a $50. I *should,* of course, subtract the AAA discount, the AARP discount, the Choice Awards discount, the Hearst Discount (none of which I remember to mention when checking in), and your Quality Inn, your Red Roof, your Super 8, your Baymont, your Hardwick Inn and Suites, your Candlewood Suites, your Staybridge Suites—all the places that may take dogs—run between $90–$130 a night. These are the joints where, leaving Lewis in the car, your advice columnist whizzes up to the front desk and says civilly, "I'd like a room for me and my dog who never sheds, never chews, never begs, never drools, never barks, never whines, and never toots."

I also, needless to say, have a tent and sleeping bag with me.

FOOD . . . . $47.00-a-day average

Breakfast is included at the hotels, and once, when I am getting Lewis's usual (two "egg patties" and whole-wheat bagel†), I witness, in the Florence, Alabama, Hardwick Inn and Suites "breakfast room," a woman with the largest calves I have ever seen in my life, wearing thick khaki shorts and a large Australian bush hat with the adjustable chin strap the size of a mastiff leash pulled very tight, digging into a stack of waffles that would have

---

* Latest Review on Hotels.com:" . . . *the price of $85 is OUTRAGEOUS for what should have been a $50 room. I have to return to Tallulah, but I'm not sure I'll be staying there. . . .*"

† Your guess, Ladies, as to what is in one of these egg patty deals is as good as mine, but if a chicken is involved, I'll eat my left bra strap. We're not talking Linda McFarland's organic Cinnamon Queen double-yolkers here. And **P.S.** Are there *any* decent bagels outside New York City? If so, please send a note to E.Jean@AskEJean.com.

fed the offensive line of a football team, and the only wonder is how this magnificent woman held back the angry white men in short-sleeved shirts in subdued stripes who are *also* hell bent on getting hold of the waffle machine and making *their* waffles before being late for *their* meetings!

The courage of the female sex—*boundless!*

P.S. Also Lewis has his Rachael Ray dog food, and I have my "emergency provisions."*

CAR REPAIRS $3,217.51

Never, certainly, in the history of the world, have there been so many detestable men causing such expense on a road trip! That Destroyer of All Comfort, Danny the Mechanic! That Disgrace of the Male Sex, Stocky Man! Those degenerates driving by in the chili-red Jester and asking if I am enjoying carnal relations with Lewis Carroll and my tripping over him and crashing headfirst into the Toyota Service parking lot and getting the two black eyes and a broken nose. Though, I don't know. The break in the nose is in the same place as ten years ago when I tripped over the dog and broke it. Then it was bumped to the left. Now it looks like it's been bumped to the right—back where it started. So maybe the clods have caused the *least* expense on a road trip. They've saved me a $9,300 surgery.

What else? I know I am forgetting items, but since I am only toting up these figures to pay homage to Madam C. J. Walker, which I think I've pulled off in fine style, I will now stop and tell you how I lost all my money when I gave my life savings to **#14** on **The Most Hideous Men of My Life List.**

---

*The aforementioned wines, cans of Amy's, packages of Purley Elizabeth's Oatmeal, etc., etc., packed in Miss Bingley's roomy underdeck storage.

Ladies, have you ever fallen for a heel?

Wait. Why am I even asking? Of course you have! What is *your* heel's name? My heel's name is Dweebie D. Fleecer.

I'm going public with our affair because, although I warn you in my column against twits, pimps, lechers, and fiends, I haven't warned you nearly enough against pin-striped polecats like Dweebie.

I break up with Dweebie because he lies, cheats, and BOY! does Dweebie neglect me! While the man is lathering my in-box with newsletters about "fourteen-year highs," my retirement account, which Dweebie promises on his website to "tailor to my individual financial objectives" and which is supposed to be increasing so I can retire one day on a glamorous spree, is leaking money. Indeed, after twenty-two years, my IRA (individual retirement account)—are you sitting down, Ladies?—had *less* money in it than at its inception!

Ladies, if I email my bank routing number to Dr. Bakare Tunde, the cousin of the Nigerian astronaut stranded in space, I'd be sitting prettier.

Oh, I know what you're thinking. You're thinking your advice columnist should never have given her hard-earned money to a sweet-talking con man who preys on helpless and pitiful ignoramuses like her.

But noooooooo. You will be astonished to hear that Dweebie is not out on bail. Dweebie is, instead, one of *Barron's* Top 100 Financial Advisors. Dweebie is on *Forbes*'s list of Top Wealth Advisors. Dweebie is quoted so many times in *The Wall Street Journal* and *The New York Times* financial pages, he is viewed as one of America's foremost chroniclers of "smart investing." Dweebie occupies a high floor of a Manhattan tower with marble floors so expensively shiny that when I step off the elevator to meet him, I can look up my *own* skirt. Which is good, because it reminds me that Dweebie Fleecer is costing me an arm and a leg.

I tape our conversation on my iPhone.

Me: I'm unhappy.
Dweeebie: I'm sorry you're unhappy.
Me: I have LESS money in my IRA than I started with twenty-two years ago.
Dweebie: Let me explain what happened.

We are in his conference room, which looks like one of the larger bathrooms in San Simeon, and it takes Dweebie forty-one minutes to tell me why my having less money in my IRA is all *my* fault. According to Dweebie, I had "called" them after the stock market crash of 2008 and "asked" them to "sell all my stocks." So my stocks were sold at a loss and my IRA has been dormant ever since. Dweebie, in other words, has been giving two flying figs about my "financial objectives."

To review: I put my little all ($50,000) into an IRA in 1996. It climbs in eight years to an undazzling $55,000. I switch to Dweebie's famous investment firm in 2004 and am doing nicely, until BOOM. Less money than when I started.

If the account had simply followed the market (after the 2008 crash, stocks showed a 16.25 percent annualized return under President Obama), I would now have over $250,000 and I'd be taking us all out for cocktails!

So the question is: Do I strike you as the kind of woman who "calls her broker"? Ladies, I don't check Miss Bingley's speedometer, I haven't been to the eye doctor in twenty years, I don't even *open* my IRA monthly statements. (**Note:** When I confess all this in my *Elle* column, the editors, appalled at my brainlessness, suggest I say it happens to a "friend" of mine.)

I don't know how big Madam C. J. Walker is, but I am waaaaay heavier than Dweebie, who tips the scales in the Ariana Grande range, and I think about giving him a running kick out his plate-glass window. But instead I will simply advise you, Ladies:

Beware the Dweebies! Check your investment accounts. Open your blasted statements! Give a standing order that no trade be made without your permission. And inquire if your Fleecer is an Accredited Investment Fiduciary. He is? Well, Ladies, it doesn't mean diddly squat. If you don't keep an eye on him, a fiduciary (a person who supposedly puts your financial interests ahead of his own) is capable of hornswoggling you as fast as a non-fiduciary.

As for me? I kissed Dweebie good-bye, transferred what was left of my IRA, and have now gone full robo. Who needs pricey financial consultants balder than Jeff Bezos when I can have egghead robots? The robots at Betterment* eliminate human judg-

---

* This is not a commercial for Betterment. They would probably pay me *not* to recommend them. Ellevest (no connection to *Elle* magazine), run by Miss Sallie

ment, follow the market as a whole, and, for fees waaaaaaay lower than Dweebie's, automatically rebalance my portfolio of index funds and ETFs and harvest my tax losses.

You already know that index funds outperform hedge funds, right, Ladies? Well. *Robots learn with every trade.* As they get smarter and smarter, you get richer and richer. How rich? I'll just say that I made more money in twelve days with robots, than I made in twelve *years* with Dweebie Fleecer.

Wow. Madam C. J. Walker is a sensation! First, she develops a theory that it is the lye—the stuff in *Drano*—in the soap women are using to wash their hair that is breaking their hair right off at the roots and causing dandruff to hail down in such large drifts that women are walking around looking like they've barely survived an avalanche. And second, she creates a shampoo called Madam Walker's Wonderful Hair Grower and gets her start "by giving myself a start," rises to employ thousands of African American women to sell her products, and inspires them to become financially independent.

What a woman!

I learn all this on the internet. There is a question, however. Is Madam C. J. Walker, who starts working in the cotton fields at age four, the first female self-made millionaire, as I have been saying? Or is Madam Walker the first female African American self-made millionaire?

Krawcheck, is another very, very good one. Women have a better track record at investing than men. Google it!

I consult the expert, Mr. John Earl Martin, the Hermione Museum curator and famous Louisiana crop duster, as he takes me on a personal tour.

Now, Mr. Martin can tell me some pretty good stories about the Theodore Roosevelt bear hunt in 1907 hosted by John Avery McIlhenny, the Tabasco hot sauce magnate, and he can tell me about the Greatest Flood in United States History when the Mississippi River sinks 27,000 square miles underwater in 1927, and he can tell me about the Battle of Milliken's Bend, and he can tell me how a wealthy and bosomy widow beguiles a railroad contractor into running new tracks past her plantation and after the line is built, she snubs him, and he can tell me how the railroad contractor, his feelings hurt, names the train depot after his old girlfriend, Tallulah, but Mr. Martin can't tell me whether Madam C. J. Walker, who is born just down the road in the little hamlet of Delta, Louisiana,* is the first female or the first African American female to make a million bucks in America.

No. Mr. Martin comes down on both sides, saying, "Madam C. J. Walker is the first female millionaire, *especially* black."

And then he stands at respectful attention in front of Madame C. J. Walker's photograph, which hangs on a wine-red wall over a fireplace mantel between two containers of flowering cotton plants.

---

* This great woman, born in 1867, died of hypertension at fifty-one. Today, a daily pill would have given her the long life she deserved. She is buried in Woodlawn Cemetery in the Bronx. She gave much of her fortune—while still alive—toward the education of African American girls, African American culture and arts, and for the anti-lynching campaigns of the NAACP.

John Earl Martin, Museum Curator and crop duster.

"What Do We Need Men For, Mr. Martin?" I say a little later in the museum tour.

Mr. Martin, who admits (after your advice columnist lifts up the hoop skirt on a mannequin and yells, "Where's this lady's underwear, sir?") that the country might "be better off" if women ran things for a while, and who has shown your advice columnist a painting of the exact positions of the rebels, the Tenth Illinois Cavalry, and the mighty African Brigade at the Battle of Millikin's Bend, takes a moment before he answers the What Do We Need Men For question.

"Well . . . " he says. "You need men to protect you."

"Against whom?"

"The enemy," says Mr. Martin, not realizing that, like the Tenth Illinois Cavalry, I am setting a trap.

"The enemy?" I say.

Mr. Martin frowns.

"You mean *other* men?" I say.

Mr. Martin, the crop-dusting celebrity—crop dusting may have begun right here in Tallulah, Ladies!—is eighty-five if he is a day, meets his wife when they are both at Tallulah High School, was "happily married for fifty years," tears up at her memory, and blows his nose. He is sprucely attired in a pair of ironed chinos with a crease, a light-blue oxford cloth short-sleeved shirt, and an Atwood Chevy-Oldsmobile baseball cap. He has just bought a new Jitterbug mobile phone "for seniors," and he and I are both astounded that it comes with about forty times more instruction than an iPhone.

"Well . . . I suppose . . . " he says warily.

"So we need men," I say, "so they can fight *other men?*"

He smiles. Mr. Martin is too smart to answer.

"But we need men to protect us?" I say. "Right?"

"Yes."

"To protect us from whom?"

Mr. Martin smiles.

"You *gotta* have protection!" he says.

"From *other* men?" I say.

"From bad men, yes," he says.

Then he adds happily:

"And from floods!"

I am at the entrance of a big pavilion that is advertised as the "Greatest Gun Show in Mississippi."

Of course, the people at the door take one gander at my jaunty Korean driving cap, Stewart hunting-plaid kilt, and the giant grosgrain bows on my three-tone saddle shoes and tell me that the "Antiques Show" is in "the pavilion next door."

"I'm here for the guns, honey," I say. "Outta my way."

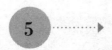

ZZZZZZ
    ZZZZZZZZZ
    "Hahahahahahahaha!"
    ZZZZZZ ZZZZZ ZZZZZZ
    ZZZZZZZZZZZZZZZZZZZZZZZ
    "LIKE THAT!"
    ZZZZZZZZZZZZZZZZZ
    "Watch out, men!" I cry.
    ZZZZZZZZZZZZZZZZZZZZZZZ
Nothing like an advice columnist running ecstatically around a gun show in a Mississippi State Fairgrounds Quonset hut want-

ing to zap every camouflage-wearing good ol' boy she sees with this here fabulous fuchsia stun gun.

"How much does this cost?" I ask.

"That one? It's $49.99."

"I love it!"

"It comes in the pink and white, the black and white, and the pink and the black."

"Look at the manicure on this girl!" I say.

Miss Kyra Johnson's nails are painted a pearly aquamarine, and Miss Kyra, a representative of Safety Products Plus, is absolutely and finally the tiniest, prettiest, sweetest, smartest, youngest, curliest-eyelashed, hoopiest-earringed, singingest little nineteen-year-old girl you can imagine. What the *hell* she is doing a few miles outside of Pearl, Mississippi, in the middle of this arsenal of shotguns, rifles, pistols, sniper rifles, assault rifles, carbines, flamethrowers, tank rippers, grenade launchers, Berettas, Colts, Glocks, and M16s, selling stun guns is a puzzle until she tells me that she is a college student, a sophomore, a "communications major," and working to pay her tuition.

Miss Kyra Johnson.

I don't know what Miss Kyra is making an hour, but, Ladies, all you have to do is look around to understand one thing:

Guns are not about protection; no, these men (and it is mostly men in balloon-seated Costco jeans and camo hats buying guns here) will somehow end up shooting their wives, each other, and themselves with the guns they're buying today for "protection." Guns are not about "protection." Guns are about money.*

"Do you take a stun gun on dates with you?" I ask.

"Yes," says Miss Kyra, who weighs all of about ninety pounds and is one of only a *very* few African Americans in this place, which, incidentally, contains more firepower than all the guns at the Battle of Vicksburg.

"So What Do We Need Men For?"

Miss Kyra drops her head and shakes it, amazed at what she is about to say.

"If we've got these," she says, holding up the zebra stunner, "pretty much nuthin'."

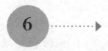

6 ··········▶

One solution to the problem of men, Ladies?
Pass a law: Only women can own guns.

---

* Men want what they can't have; and not to get into it, but the gun manufacturers are probably making more $$$ *because* of the threats of gun control.

Just before they ask your advice columnist to "leave" the "Greatest Gun Show in Mississippi" for the appalling atrocity of "videotaping" Miss Kyra Johnson and accidently capturing a bunch of Mississippi's cultural leaders not looking their best, I ask a nice, smiling young chap outfitted from head to boots in camouflage who has his two little kids with him also bundled into camouflage—and indeed there is so much camouflage going on in this place I'm surprised I can see *anyone*—what he is looking for when purchasing a gun?

He grins and says:

"I'm just looking for something to protect my family."

"From whom?" I say.

"What?" he says.

"From whom are you protecting your family?"

"Well . . . " he says.

"Are you buying a gun to protect your family from that guy over there who is buying a gun?"

"No," he says. "I'm looking to protect myself from interviewers."

"Wait. From interviewers?"

"*Intruders,*" he says, smiling, and this is about the point when they come to escort Auntie Eeee from the premises.

Ladies, I hope you have another travel book handy with descriptions of the towns we've been visiting. A book listing the homes of the "notable citizens"* and the pleasant walks round and about Pearl, Mississippi, would be nice, for instance, because I can't tell you a single thing about Pearl, Mississippi, as my whole purpose for living is to ask people What Do We Need Men For, and then, if we decide we don't need them, to do away with them. Also I like venting my spleen and showing my loathing for **The Most Hideous Men of My Life.**

In short, I stay inside my Candlewood Suites room ("with kitchenette!") and only come out to go to the "Greatest Gun Show in Mississippi," which is not even *in* Pearl, by the way, but ten minutes away, and now that they have kicked your advice columnist out of *that,* I walk to the parking lot, check on Lewis, who is happily asleep in Miss Bingley's back seat, and stroll on toward the Mississippi State Fairgrounds Coliseum where the big cutting horse contest is going on.

But little did I dare hope to see such glamour in the Magnolia State!

For standing beside a long, glistening white horse trailer,

---

* Bianca Knight—track athlete
Tommy Aldridge—drummer
Justin Jenkins—Buffalo Bills player
George Kersh—athlete
Ty Tabor—singer, guitarist for King's X
Eric Washington—former NBA player
Thank you, *Wikipedia!*

pulled by a big black three-quarter-ton Chevy truck, stands a chestnut horse so comely, with a rump so big and glossy, and a face so startlingly intelligent, he looks like he has debouched from a private jet just in from the Land of the Houyhnhnms.

"*Who* is this?" I say, toddling over.

"Sammy."

"Hello, Sammy!"

"Official name Sweet Revenge."

"Sweet Revenge—wait," I say to the young woman saddling him. "You mean, hold on—*Sweet Reyvenge?* You're *kidding!* I've been reading about you!"

You see, Ladies? Lollygagging around your hotel room ("with kitchenette!") eating oatmeal, airing the five kilts, beetling around the internet, and accidentally discovering that the Southern Cutting Horse Futurity is happening *next to the gun show* is twice as fun as driving all over godforsaken Pearl!

"So *you* must be—" I say to the young woman. "I'm sorry; I just read about you and watched some videos, and I can't . . ." The bucket-of-cream complexion, the green eyes, the merry smile . . .

"Lauren Middleton."

HA! Only one of *the* top amateur cutting horse competitors in America! Hang on. As we've been talking about money, Ladies, let's look up Lauren Middleton's winnings to date:

Damnnnnn! $715,000!*

"What Do We Need Men For, Miss Lauren?" I say.

"We have to get to the point," she says, tightening the front cinch on Sammy's saddle, "where we don't *need* them."

"And if we could put all the men somewhere so we could run things for a while," I say, "where would be a good place to put them?"

---

* Cutting horse competitions are one of the few sports where men and women compete with and against one another and win equal—repeat, *equal*—prize money.

She looks up from buckling the rear cinch.

"We could put the men, like in some sort of . . ." She stops and considers. "Like some sort of *school*," she says, running her hand over Sammy's glorious rump.

"And then we women could run the world!" I say.

Lauren Middleton and Sammy.

"And the men would go to school," says Miss Lauren, kneeling down and putting a brace on Sammy's left back leg. "They would get some counseling, or maybe not counseling, you know what I mean, some *direction,* and when they come out, we women will have made the world a better place. And so the men will be happier. Because *ultimately,* men want to be taken care of by women. Which is funny. They don't want us to be powerful, but they want us to take *care* of them."

"Oh!" I cry.

This is a new idea to me and I am elated. "You're right! Men want to be taken care of!"

"Yup," says Miss Lauren. "They do."

"Well, then, why don't they give us equal pay so that we can take care of them *better?*"

"They haven't figured that one out yet," says Miss Lauren, who goes on to win here tonight in Mississippi and then, Ladies, she and Sammy gallop onto the pages of history. They triumph at the big one: The National Cutting Horse Finals in Fort Worth, Texas. Congratulations, Lauren, and *YeeeeeeeeHa*!

We are heading to Verona, Mississippi, beauty capital of the world, but it is Saturday afternoon in Tupelo (#11,388 most popular girl's name), and wedding parties are fluttering about the Elvis Presley birthplace, the Elvis Presley Memorial Chapel, the Elvis Presley Story Wall, the Elvis Presley Fountain of Life, the Elvis Presley Museum, the Elvis Presley Theater, the Elvis Presley Bridge Over Troubled Waters, the Elvis Presley Gift Shop, and the Elvis Presley Restrooms, so Lewis and I park Miss Bingley and run up to a fetching group of bridesmaids in peach.

"Ladies!" I cry. "How spectacular you are! What Do We Need Men For?"

"Nothing," says the maid of honor, a real head-turner with tattoos of bloodred jungle flowers running up her left arm. "I just got divorced!"

I turn to the bride and say:

"Do you *need* a husband?"

"Oh, no!" she says. "I just want him for the fun, so I struck 'obey' from the vows."

Anna Jade Nguyen fixing the bride's hair.

10 ··········▶

If they ever held a mud-wrestling championship between Estée Lauder, Elizabeth Arden, and Madam C. J. Walker, the House of Beauty, just off Seventh Street in Verona, Mississippi, would be the place to hold it.*

Audrey Morgan (left) with Cheri Jamison, the new proprietress of the House of Beauty.

---

* Elvis's parents eloped to Verona, and I like to picture Elvis's mother, the twenty-one-year-old looker Gladys Smith, and the seventeen-year-old Vernon Presley spending the night in the House of Beauty.

Famous as a local pulchritudinous enterprise, the inside of the House of Beauty looks like a Harvard Business School experiment if the Harvard Business School had hired Hieronymus Bosch to decorate the premises with every beauty implement known to womankind since 1699.

The new proprietress, Miss Cheri (chic accent on the last two letters) Jamison, invites me in. She wears a lovely, low, squared-off pompadour and says she "doesn't need men." But her friend Miss Audrey Morgan, a short, pretty woman with a braids-and-bouffant, gold hoops, a red Ed Hardy T-shirt, and a degree from one of the South's fanciest colleges, delivers such a passionate opposing argument on why we *do* need men ("family structure," "helping little girls understand their place in the world," and so forth) I feel it my duty to remind Miss Audrey how much less money women in Verona earn as compared to men* and how *ridiculously* less money some African American women earn, and how even Susan B. Anthony and Frederick Douglass (a feminist down to his very liver) concluded that as they couldn't get the US Congress to give the vote to women *and* to black men in 1870, they decided to let the "women wait" another fifty years, or rather, ninety years, as many African American and Native American women in places like Verona, Mississippi, were prevented from voting until the 1960s.†

Miss Audrey is sitting next to Miss Cheri on the House of Beauty love seat, and her facial muscles are popping and sparking the whole time I'm yakking, and finally, no longer able to help herself, she slams her fist down on the love seat with such force that Miss Cheri is almost bounced off onto the floor.

"*This has got to stop!*" cries Miss Audrey.

---

* According to the 2000 census, males had a median income of $25,000 versus $18,305 for females.

† And women voters in places like Indiana, Georgia, North Dakota, etc., are *still* suppressed.

Miss Priscilla Owens, Miss Cheri's and Miss Audrey's friend, a calm woman with a perfect pageboy, pulls her own chair out of Miss Audrey's way.

"It's *disgusting!*" says Miss Audrey. "As much as we women do! Working two jobs! Taking care of the kids! Cooking! The laundry! Doing everything we can to make ends meet—and still *nothing. We're still waiting!*"

"We're being held in our place!" says Miss Priscilla.

"We need more money!" says Miss Audrey. "More jobs. Affordable housing *as a right!* More investment in women!"

"Miss Audrey," I say, laughing, as the light zings off a collection of straightening irons so vast that if they were all plugged in, they would straighten every curl, kink, crimp, wave, swirl, and ringlet in the whole state of Mississippi, not to mention Louisiana. "Listen to yourself. Are you thinking of—"

"Yes!" she says. "I'm gonna run for mayor of Verona!"

Ladies, do you miss the scenery on this road trip? Do you long for a lyrical description of that carpet of crocus? That cow chewing her cud? Send me a note on ejeancarroll.com. Name the forest, field, farmhouse, village, lake, river, moose, mountain, molehill, etc., you would like described, and I will call you back and describe it. OK? Otherwise, I quite detest scenery in books. Alluring depictions of the shrubbery penned by the Holy Trinity—Jane, Charlotte, and George?* Bah! Sketches of countrysides? Phooey!

---

* Austen, Brontë, Eliot.

Landscapes? Ha! No scenery here, if you please, Ladies. If a genius like Rachel Cusk can write three novels that contain *no action*, I can write one road trip book that contains *no scenery*.

So what do I do between Tupelo (the brides) and Verona (the House of Beauty), a distance of 5.8 miles through roly-poly hills, if I am *not* making notes about scenery? Well, first, I pull over. And I sit gazing and smiling at a photo that my neighbor, Eileen Bertelli, texts me of Vagina T. Fireball wearing the red-blue-green-yellow Carmen Miranda collar I made her.

The Carmen Miranda helps songbirds spot Vagina T. when she's outside hunting—lurking behind a fern—the little twat! Since she's been wearing it, she has not caught one bird. Here's a side-angle shot of the Carmen Miranda I took.

Which gives me a notion. Why don't we just put men in collars, Ladies? Red for harassers. Blue for cheaters. Green for men who pay women less. Yellow for men who push back against our rising power, and so on. The collars should be about four feet in diameter and light up at night.

Also between Tupelo and Verona, I do exercises. You exercise in your vehicles too, right, Ladies? You do your steering-wheel isometrics, your neck rolls, your torso twists. Please join me for this *special* workout.

The What Do We Need Men For Road Trip Exercises

As one never knows when one will run into a harasser like **#15** on **The Most Hideous Men of My Life List**—the Jolly Octopus: Les Moonves, chairman of the board, president, and chief executive officer of the CBS Corporation*—one must stay in tip-top condition.

---

* As I do not want to dignify this chump by putting his history in the text, here he is in a footnote—though, Ladies, I think you probably know *all about* Mr. Moonves. Rumors of a highly discreditable nature have been roaring through New York and LA for *years* about Moonves—so much so that I remember in 2001 I was dining at Elaine's with two women, a big-deal *New York Times* writer and a glamorous movie star—each pursuing a different career, each living in a different city—and *both* had personal, emotionally shattering Moonves stories.

For two decades, reporters had tried and failed to establish proof of Moonves's sexual misconduct. He was so powerful himself, and so protected by the Hollywood Boys Club, he seemed untouchable. And then Mr. Ronan Farrow, honored with the Pulitzer for his reporting of the sexual assault allegations brought against Harvey Weinstein—shared with Miss Jodi Kantor and Miss Megan Twohey of *The New York Times*—broke the Moonves story in *The New Yorker.* Six women told their stories about Moonves's sexual dereliction to Farrow *on the record*.

Any other man would have been forced to resign. Not Moonves. He dined out with his wife, reality and talk show host Julie Chen, at Nobu Malibu—the trough for LA power players—and just when it looked like Moonves had climbed on the steps of his dead self and made it back on top, Farrow socked him with a second piece in *The New Yorker.* It was so devastating—Moonves forcing women to perform fellatio, etc., etc.—the man stepped down within eight hours of it appearing online.

He was down . . . but not out. He denied it all. The CBS board was—incredibly!—considering giving him a $120 million severance when Rachel Abrams and Edmund Lee of *The New York Times* published a story revealing that investigators hired by CBS had determined that Moonves, to save his $120 million deal, had destroyed evidence and misled them. The investigators also reported allegations that a CBS employee was "on call" to perform oral sex on Mr. Moonves. On December 17, 2018, the CBS Corporation, half-dead from embarrassment, declared that Les Moonves would be fired "for cause." I.e., The Octopus continued to deny, deny, deny, but will not get the $120 million. May I stop writing about him now in this footnote? I am sick to my stomach.

The Push-Up. To tone arms, put car into neutral. Get out. Walk around to rear. Push car down road.

The Buttock Clench. Turn up Lady Gaga. With both hands on wheel—going no faster than eighty-eight miles per hour—squeeze right buttock five times with Gaga's beat. Squeeze left buttock five times with Gaga's beat. Squeeze left and right buttocks together to Gaga's beat. Squeeze right buttock then left buttock then right buttock then left buttock then right buttock then left buttock then right buttock then left buttock until arriving at destination. If you can still walk, your fanny will look like the bouncing basketballs at a Golden State Warriors free throw practice.

The Face Firmer. To eliminate that droopy jawline, picture Les Moonves. He is a shortish chap with two eyes and a beak. He once earned $69 million a year. Now imagine him plunging around an elevator in the Hotel Nikko in Beverly Hills chasing your advice columnist. Your screams will tighten all facial muscles.

I had been interviewing Moonves in the lounge of the Nikko lobby for an *Esquire* story,* and apparently one look at me—a fiftysomething journalist in a pair of old brown-and-beige oxfords—and Moonves's life isn't his own.

---

* "Dangerous Minds," *Esquire,* February 1997.

When the interview is finished (and for a man like Moonves, talking about himself for an hour and a half is as good as downing two gallons of Spanish fly), he follows me to the elevator, and when I turn to say goodbye, he says:

"You're smart."

I say:

"Thank you!"

He says:

"Smart enough to choose an out-of-the-way hotel," and he steps into the elevator behind me and, his pants bursting with demands, presses the door closed and goes at me like an octopus.

I don't know how many apertures and openings *you* possess, Ladies, but Moonves, with his arms squirming and poking and goosing and scooping and pricking and pulling and prodding and jabbing, is looking for fissures I don't even know I own, and—by God!—I am not certain that even if I pull *off* one of his arms, it won't crawl after me and attack me in my hotel bed. Hell, I am thrilled I escape before he expels his ink!

Naturally, I do not mention this in the article. With two exceptions, I do not mention anything about Moonves to anyone.

IX

"Opportunity Is a Beautiful Woman. You Have to Grab Her."*

Florence, Alabama
(#841 Most Popular Girl's Name)

Bonnieville, Kentucky
(#709 Most Popular Girl's Name)

---

* Recording of Helen Keller, Helen Keller Birthplace

Ladies, I can't move, can't turn my head, can't bend my elbows, can't waggle my wrists, can't roll my shoulders, can't raise my arms, can't bend my knees, can't tilt my toes, can't lift my legs . . .

I am in a queen-size bed in a Florence, Alabama, Hardwick Inn and Suites. The microwave clock says 3:47 A.M. The room is dark—the room is so dark it is glittering. Lewis is here. He is doing his best *clak-clak*s to keep my spirits up. But you know those knobs on the backs of your necks, Ladies? Mine are disintegrating one at a time, minute by minute. Moving my head is out of the question. If my neck did not hurt so much,* I wouldn't mind—not mind at all— being unable to move—because I love a motel bed. I love a motel bed five times more than I love my own bed. I love a motel bed because if I am in a motel bed, it means I am on a *story,* and when I am on a story, I am the happiest girl in the world.

I have ranked my favorites:

The Number One Most Memorable Motel Bed of My Career is not a bed. And it is not in a motel. It is a sleeping bag in a tent in the Shawangunk Mountains.

---

* This is the *obvious* symptom of what is going wrong with my body, though I could not know it at the time.

The year is 1982. I, E. Jean Carroll, a nobody, an insect, an amoeba who has published one little thing in *Esquire,* am calling the most powerful literary agent in New York:

"Mr. Mort Janklow! Hello! I would like to take your client, Miss Fran Lebowitz, camping for *Outside* magazine."

"Ha ha ha ha ha."

"Hello? Mr. Jank—?"

"How much?"

"How much what?"

"How much are you paying her?"

"We do not pay for stories, Mr. Janklow. *Outside* is a magazine."

"Ha ha ha ha ha ha."

"Mr.—"

"Fran Lebowitz does not *go* outside," said Mr. Janklow, and, laughing, he hung up.

Fran Lebowitz *did* happen to describe the outdoors as a "place you must pass through in order to get from your apartment into a taxicab," and she *did* mention once that the sun was "the sort of harsh overhead lighting that is so unflattering to the heavy smoker"; but, I was chock-full of pizzzaazzz! *Outside* was the new hot thing. It would soon hog the National Magazine Awards. I was daffy with belief in myself. I put down the phone and picked up my issue of *Vogue.* Inside was a photograph of Fran Lebowitz lying on her bed doing what she is world-famous for doing—

talking on the phone. It was, of course, a rotary phone. I could read on the dial, if I used a magnifying glass, Fran Lebowitz's phone number.

"Hello! Miss Lebowitz!"

"Yes."

"Miss Lebowitz! I would like to take you camping for *Outside* magazine! Leave your sofa, Miss Lebowitz! Leave your apartment! Let's go camping! It'll be a riot!"

"Who is this?"

"I'm a writer for *Outside* magazine, E. Jean Carroll. Hello! Hello! The whole world will love it! Imagine! Fran Lebowitz leaves Greenwich Village! Fran Lebowitz goes *camping!*"

"When?"

"Whenever you can get three days free. How about the weekend of the eighteenth?"

"All right. Yes. Thank you for inviting me."

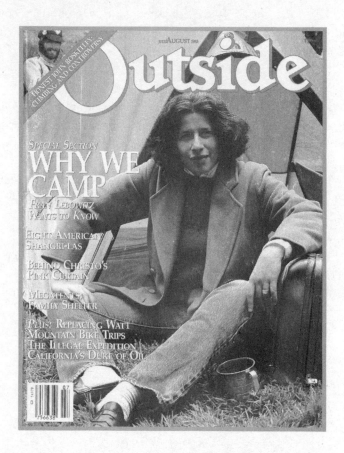

I later interviewed Fran for *Playboy*,* and we talked about men and how Fran would like to marry "a very rich dead man," and then I asked if a woman's purpose in life was to find the perfect man. Fran said no. A woman's quest in life should be to find the perfect apartment.

---

* "Twenty Questions: Fran Lebowitz," *Playboy*, July 1984.

The daily routine of that icon of Twentieth-Century Debauchery and Journalism—Hunter S. Thompson:

3:00 p.m. rise
3:05 Chivas Regal with the morning papers, Dunhills
3:45 cocaine
3:50 another glass of Chivas, Dunhill
4:05 first cup of coffee, Dunhill
4:15 cocaine
4:16 orange juice, Dunhill
4:30 cocaine
4:54 cocaine
5:05 cocaine
5:11 coffee, Dunhill
5:30 more ice in the Chivas
5:45 cocaine, etc., etc.
6:00 grass to take the edge off the day
7:00 Woody Creek Tavern for lunch—Heineken, two margaritas,
   two cheeseburgers, two orders of fries, a plate of tomatoes,
   coleslaw, a taco salad, a double order of fried onion rings, carrot
   cake, ice cream, a bean fritter, Dunhills, another Heineken,
   cocaine, and, for the ride home, a snow cone (a glass of shredded
   ice over which is poured three or four jiggers of Chivas)
9:00 starts snorting cocaine seriously
10:00 drops acid
11:00 Chartreuse, cocaine, grass

11:30 cocaine, etc., etc.
12:00 midnight, Hunter S. Thompson is ready to write.
12:05–6:00 a.m. Chartreuse, cocaine, grass, Chivas, coffee,
    Heineken, clove cigarettes, grapefruit, Dunhills, orange juice, gin,
    continuous pornographic movies
6:00 the hot tub—champagne, Dove Bars, fettuccine Alfredo
8:00 Halcyon
*8:20 sleep**

Hence, the Number Two Most Memorable Motel Bed of My Career is a Mayflower Hotel bed and stars Hunter. Hunter lived at his ranch, Owl Farm, outside Woody Creek, Colorado; but he came to New York often, and we would pal around—go to Elaine's, hang out at strip clubs, live sex shows, and so on. As I mentioned in the biography, one night, Hunter called me howling and moaning into the phone about two red-haired "Malaysian strumpets" who were covering him—as he spoke!—from head to foot in Gillette Foamy and were about to shave every hair off his body up to and including his eyebrows. He wanted me to come over immediately and supervise.

He was staying in a suite at the Mayflower Hotel on Central Park West under the name of Mr. Walker. He greeted me wearing a shade of Mandrill-pink lipstick that I found so fetching I later purchased a tube myself.

It soon transpired that the reason Hunter called me was *not* to supervise the trollops (they'd already departed—leaving water all over the floor) but because Bob Wallace, the editor of *Rolling Stone* (who was also my editor and refused to print the word *cunt* in the opening of my Billy Idol piece, remarking: "E. Jean, when Richard Nixon calls you a cunt, I will happily print it, but when Billy Idol calls you a cunt, we will use an em dash"), was coming the next day

---

* From page one of my biography, *Hunter: The Strange and Savage Life of Hunter. S. Thompson* (New York: Dutton, 1993).

to pick up Hunter's Vietnam piece, which *Rolling Stone* was running, in a fit of Hunter Love, ten years or so after the evacuation.

Hunter and I watched a game on TV, washed out his laundry (Hunter was the cleanest man I have ever met), worked on the piece, lined up sugar cubes "for the CIA" at the empty tables in the Conservatory restaurant (I can't remember if we were "warning" the CIA of a plot or "foiling" a CIA plot), rode up and down in the elevator, ran back and forth in the hallway, ordered room service, and ate it on that Mayflower hotel bed. I was just finishing a tin-roof ice cream sundae when the notion of writing a biography about Hunter occurred to me.

When Wallace arrived with an assistant (sometimes two assistants were required to prepare a Hunter Thompson piece for publication on account of the weeping and screeching—not all of it Hunter's), Hunter handed him the nearly finished article. I'll never forget the flabbergasted look on Wallace's face.

Later, I surprised Hunter by flying to Colorado on his birthday, calling and *telling* him that I was writing his biography, and to come get me; I was at the Woody Creek Tavern.

He arrived in his glistening fire-apple-red Pontiac, with the big top *down*. A Duke if I ever saw one! I turned on my tape recorder, got in the car, and rarely turned the tape recorder *off* until several days later when we got into a fistfight at 3:30 in the morning—I am a member of the Carla Club, when a fellow hits me, I hit back, but a girl can only take so much—and I ran to the phone to call a taxi.

I dialed.

Hunter put his finger on the button.

I dialed again.

Hunter put his finger on the button.

I dialed again.

A nice lady at the taxi service said, "Hello."

"Help! Help! Come and get me!" I screamed.

"Are you at Hunter's?" said the lady.

The Number Three Most Memorable Motel Bed of My Career, also not a motel bed, is my old bed—circa 1965—in the "cold dorm" of the big, long, white, three-story, Tara-esque Pi Beta Phi sorority house, where I slept for eight days when I went back to Indiana University in Bloomington, Indiana, in 1983 to go through rush. The outgoing president of the house argued like Clarence Darrow at the Scopes Monkey Trial against my being allowed in the house during rush, let alone being permitted to record the hash sessions. (Hash: A nightly bloodbath where sorority members discuss and vote on young women who *want* to be sorority members.)

But was I not royalty? Did I not wear the Miss IU Crown? Did I not carry the Miss Cheerleader USA scepter? Was that not my gigantic, huge photo hanging in the IU Student Union? Did I not arrive and buy the sisters so many drinks at the Regulator that Betsy barfed on the floor? The house took a vote. I was in.

And, boy, was I shocked! Hash sessions were brutal when I was a Pi Phi. My imbecilic sisters once voted down a beautiful, witty Japanese American girl with a 3.8 and an athletic scholarship because several girls in the house said their fathers, who fought against Japan in World War II, "might not like to see a Japanese person." *Their fathers!* I should have banged their heads together on the spot!*

---

* One of the fathers, I later learned, had sexually assaulted his daughter repeatedly until she went to college.

And the smarter, wiser, more politically hip young women I featured in my story two decades later? How did they behave in hash? My God! It was like watching female baboons discharge their excrement upon the innocent. The "discussion" was so anti-female, so cruel ("I can't see that doggy-lookin' broad in a Pi Phi sweatshirt," etc., etc.), I could not understand why anyone would want to *be* in a sorority in 1983.

The piece ran in *Playgirl*—a sly, rebellious magazine of the '70s and '80s that fought for freedom of choice and equal rights, and featured semi-nude men in response to the naked women in *Playboy*. The national leadership of Pi Phi read the piece, and, after snapping their cami-knickers, sent me the following letter:

FROM: Grand President, Jean Wirths Scott (Mrs. Jon)
To: E. Jean Carroll

Dear Jean,
At the most recent meeting of the Grand Council of Pi Beta Phi, your status as a member of the [sorority] was discussed. The discussion, as you might guess, was brought about by the article you wrote ["Sorority Sisters"] in which discredit was reflected on the Indiana Beta chapter of Pi Beta Phi and on the name of Pi Beta Phi in general . . . [etc., etc., etc.]

The letter concludes, I am delighted to say, Ladies, with the announcement that the Grand Council of Pi Beta Phi had voted your advice columnist *out*.

P.S. I remember wearing my black jeans, my banana-colored cowgirl boots, my Chinese wrapper, my black corduroy shirt, my black leather vest, my white cheerleading sweater, my buckskin jacket with the fringe, and carrying my purple Crown Royal bag with gold tassels as a purse while staying in the Pi Phi house. I remember so clearly because my black jeans, banana-colored cowgirl boots, Chinese wrapper, black corduroy shirt, black leather vest, white cheerleading sweater, buckskin jacket with the fringe, and purple Crown Royal bag were almost the only things to wear that I owned. I wore them in San Francisco when I covered the People Who Thought They Were Too Good-Looking, and they guessed that I should be rated "a six and a half, *maybe* a seven." I wore them when I covered cheerleading tryouts at UCLA. I wore them when I was reporting a story about an XXX movie shoot, and every time I walked onto the set with my tape recorder and notebook, the director stopped what he was doing, threw open his arms, and cried ecstatically, "Oh, my darling! Every time I see you, I get erect!"

I wore them when I covered the Miss Rodeo America competition in Oklahoma City when Miss Utah was harnessed in a baby-blue western suit, baby-blue boots, white ruffled blouse, baby-blue cowboy hat, and clasped her Miss Rodeo Utah purse in her baby-blue gloves.

Here is a photo of the black corduroy shirt, black leather vest, and lace handkerchief I was affecting at the time. You can admire it, the Chinese wrapper, and banana-colored cowgirl boots in the documentary *Where the Heart Roams,* directed by George Paul Csicsery. I was wearing them as I traveled across the nation with the bestselling romance writers in America on the "Love Train." Barbara Cartland, the Queen of Romance, met us at Penn Station wearing a hot-pink pillbox with two sprays of ostrich feathers coming out the top. I was so excited about doing this story I paid my own way out to LA to get on the train!

P.P.S. Where I *lived* was even more fantastically glamorous than what I wore. After taking Fran camping and returning her to Manhattan, I had ridden a Greyhound bus back to Montana, gathered up my stuff, collected Tits, the cattle dog, Big T, the three-legged cat, and Tee-Tony, the marmalade feline, threw in a couple of sawhorses, some lumber, and six bales of hay, said adios to my husband, Steve, a great and marvelous man—just because it ends doesn't mean it fails—and, leaving Montana at midnight, drove a U-Haul that didn't start unless it was rolling down a hill back to New York and to the apartment I had rented for $400 a month on West Twenty-sixth street.

Ladies! The first floor of the Metropolitan Museum of Art was *nothing* to it. The architectural highlight of my new premises—aside from the fact that it was located beneath a family of fortune-tellers—was its dirt floors. Tits could bury her bones in the living room. I had no bathtub, no shower, no kitchen. I washed in a basement basin. I made furniture out of the bales of hay and sawhorses.

"*Who* is your decorator?" said Richard Harris, walking into the joint and stopping dead in his tracks. *Stunned* is the word.*

The Number Four Most Memorable Motel Bed of My Career: all the motel beds I slept in when I hit the road for *Esquire* and visited my old boyfriends.† Yes, I have not totally loathed many a man in my day, Ladies.

The illustrious, funny, brilliant Jennifer Jason Leigh (who, I must say, single-handedly saved Quentin Tarantino's *Hateful Eight*) was doing research for her role as a journalist in the movie *Dolores Claiborne* and was trailing me around *Esquire*. She sat in on an edit session. But she didn't just sit. When Bill Tonelli, my editor and friend, suggested a (small—three-line) cut in the article we were editing, Miss Jennifer *blasted* Tonelli like she was Dorothy Parker (which, come to think of it, she *was* Dorothy

---

* Ladies, I know you are younger than I am, but I don't need to tell you who Richard Harris is, do I? King Arthur in *Camelot?* Marcus Aurelius in *Gladiator*, Albus Dumbledore in *Harry Potter?*

† "Loves of My Life," *Esquire*, June 1995.

Parker in the movie *Mrs. Parker and the Vicious Circle*). The three lines stayed in! I've never been happier in my life than the years I was at *Esquire* with Tonelli, David Hirshey, Michael Solomon, Will Blythe, Terry McDonell, Ed Kosner—my God! *There's* a list of likable rogues! It is almost enough to make me, who wants to get rid of men, think of keeping a few. Would your advice columnist look weak if she added to the list Rob Fleder at *Sports Illustrated*. Am I going daft?

The Number Five Most Memorable Motel Bed of My Career is the hotel bed sketch titled "Room Service" I wrote for *Saturday Night Live*. Like 90 percent of my sketches, it didn't make it to air. However, after discarding it, the producer, Lorne Michaels, in a desperate bind to find a host for the upcoming show, sent me to Boston to cajole the great baseball player Reggie Jackson (Mr. October) into hosting the show that very Saturday night.

This was in the era *after* Garrett Morris and *before* Maya Rudolph, Leslie Jones, Eddie Murphy, Chris Rock, etc., etc., when *SNL* had no African American writers, no African American producers, no African American scenery builders, no African American costumers, no African American hair-and-makeup people, and no African American actors. Lorne sent me, I guess, because I was boffing an African American.

He also sent Dennis Miller, the Weekend Update anchor, whose knowledge of baseball was so great that he could have made a living in saloons winning bets. Dennis and I met Mr. Jackson—his mustache bristling like an egg whisk, his muscles popping, his wit flowing—in the visiting team dugout at Fenway Park. He was in a pennant race at the time, expecting to win his sixth or seventh World Series ring, and though it is not my intention to reveal the distresses Mr. October caused the show by turning us down, I will say that Dennis and I had such a good time on the plane going home telling each other about our sex lives that when it landed we made a pact never, *never* to speak of it again.

The Number Six Most Memorable Motel Bed of My Career is in a motel in Dryden, New York, a lovely and treacherous little hamlet in the Finger Lakes region. It is the home of Dryden High School and the Dryden High football team, the mighty Purple Lions. I was gathering facts for "The Cheerleaders,"* the story of the torture and murder of two Purple Lions cheerleaders, the suicide by hanging of the man who killed them, the death in a car accident of the Purple Lions football star, the suicide of the star's best friend (also a Purple Lions football player), the murder of the Purple Lions football coach, the suicide of the boy who killed the football coach at the grave of his ex-girlfriend who had also killed herself, and the fiery death of the third and most popular cheerleader.

I wrote the story for *Rolling Stone*. Jann Wenner, the editor in chief, said it was "too bloody." I sold it to *Spin*. It went on to be selected for *Best American Crime Writing: 2002 Edition*. Fifteen or sixteen film companies have tried to option it—the husband of a

---

* "The Cheerleaders," *Spin,* 2001.

famous movie star called me just this year, excited to make a movie. I turn them all down. The story, you see, centers on my beautiful niece Tiffany Starr, the captain of the cheerleaders and daughter of the football coach. She is now a social worker, happily married to my nephew Berry Blanton, a creative director, and they have a brilliant young son.

Roger Ailes once interviewed me for a job. He was creating a new network from scratch for NBC called America's Talking. (It later became MSNBC.) Toward the end of the interview, he asked, "What's your biggest flaw, E. Jean?"

I was so startled to hear the renegade broadcaster asking this old chestnut, I blurted out:

"Oh, HEAVENS! I'm hopeless! I'm pathetic! I can't make an omelet. I have no hand-eye coordination. I never take vacations. I completely overdo everything. I detest all other advice columnists. I don't like men in Speedos. I worry too much about every person who writes to my column. I hate people who kill mice. My temperature is 96.1. I think suffering for love is stupid. I haven't been to a hairdresser in three years. I'm fighting the weight of gravity. I dance forward instead of backward in salsa. I'm terrified of looking in the mirror. You won't understand the whole mirror deal until you're my age, Mr. Ailes—*oh!*—you *are* my age? No way, Mr. Ailes! Getouttahere! What's your secret, swear to God, you look thirty-eight—" and so on.

To shut me up, Roger gave me my own TV show.

Ask E. Jean was a live, daily, one-hour frolic that *Entertain-*

ment Weekly called "America's Answering Machine." Men and women would sit on the Ask Eeee sofa and tell me their problems, and their problems were usually so interesting, so tragic, so comic, or so harrowing (about their careers, romances, weight, finances, friendships gone bad, etc.) that viewers at home could put their own problems into perspective, and everybody felt *better*. TV critics loved it because I jumped up and down on the sofa, harangued people, snorted like a rhino, took live calls, cried with guests whose hearts were breaking, and never sugarcoated my advice, and Ladies, it was *stupendous!*

Because of its time slot (4:00 P.M. with a rerun at 11:00 P.M.), we received lots of questions from women who had very young children and were too "exhausted" to want sex with their husbands. We also received lots of questions from women who had very young children and weren't having *enough* sex with their husbands. My advice was the same. Get a babysitter, go to a motel, pull down the blinds, and nap! When you wake up, you'll enjoy *fabulous sex!*

I must have dragged the covers off that Number Seven Most Memorable Motel Bed two or three times a month.

This was Love in the Time of Roger Ailes.

Egads! How I adored that man!

I loved him from the moment I saw his fat, smiling face. He would come down from his office before my show and put his bald, golden-pink, flubbery head just inside my dressing room. I would come to the door with my hair in curlers the size of coffee cans, and he would make a muscle for me and ask what the topic of today's show was and give me such a big boost of confidence that I thought I was Queen Nefertiti. Roger was the most buoyant, turbulent, warlike optimist I ever met! I am talking of love for a friend here, not romantic love.

I adored the man so much that one day shortly after America's Talking became MSNBC and Roger began creating Fox News, he invited me to lunch (just the two of us!) at Le Cirque. I was

running late, booming into town from Nyack, anxiously zigzag-
ging down Amsterdam Avenue or Broadway, I can't remember
which, in Harlem, and a cop pulled me over for speeding.

"Hello, Officer!" I sang out.

I was behind the wheel of my daffodil-yellow, 1961 Cadillac
convertible. (A Queen!)

"License and registration, please," he said.

"Yes, sir!"

I handed them over.

He was sauntering back to his patrol car with them when he
got a call, and, shouting at me, "DON'T MOVE!" he lunged
into his vehicle and drove off with his siren flaring. I put the
Queen in gear, and waving "so long" to the kids who had gathered round hoping for an amusing scene with New York's Finest,
I balled the jack to midtown to meet Roger. I made it on time,
and by God! We ate like Circe's pigs!*

---

* From the hilarious ribbing I took when I ducked into the—I believe it was the
Twenty-eighth Precinct—to retrieve my driver's license and registration, I think the cop
must have let me off. I don't remember paying a fine.

I was definitely let off when I was stopped by a cop for going the wrong way on
a one-way road on the journey home from Roger's lake cottage in Sparta a short time
later. "Have you been drinkin' tonight?" said the cop, leaning in the window to catch
any smell of alcohol. "HEAVENS, NO! Officer!" I cried. "But if you happen to have
any wine," I added, "please pour me a drink. I've been listening to Roger Ailes rant all
night about the Clintons!"

The *Ask E. Jean* show.

10 ············▶

Here is Lewis. He stands by the Florence, Alabama, Hardwick Inn bed staring at me as if his whole life has been leading up to this moment. The sun is pouring itself into the murk of our room through slits in the curtains. I have occupied the last three hours lying flat on the bed, loosening up my joints, one by one, like Samuel Beckett's old lady in her bath—ankles, knees, hips, elbows, wrists, etc. The trick, now, will be to stand up.

I am on the far right side of the bed. My neck has been replaced with a sock full of needles. One of the needles is stabbing me because I have gone so far as to *think* of sitting up. So the plan is to lift my left leg, roll it over my right leg toward the floor, aim my left foot down, down, down, nudging my body over the edge of the bed, touch my foot down on the carpet, and let my body fall in a slow rolling descent over my bended knee . . . and then, stand up. This is a combination of two high-jump techniques: the western roll and the straddle. I messed up the straddle probably 150 times in my high jump career, but here goes.

"Fuuuuuuuuuuuuuuuuuuuck!"

I forgot my own rule: NEVER REMOVE YOUR SHOES IN A HARDWICK INN AND SUITES.

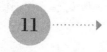

Your advice columnist has made it *out of the room,* Ladies!*

---

*Though later, no doctor would believe it. After I got home from the What Do We Need Men For trip, and after weeks in the hospital with my "mystery" condition, the editor of this book, Elisabeth Dyssegaard, recommended I see Dr. Jeffrey Greene, clinical professor of medicine at NYU Langone. Dr. Greene diagnosed probable AOSD—adult-onset Still's disease—a rare condition in which one's autoimmune system attacks one's healthy organs. This little attack in Florence may have been the first shot across the bow.

P.S. I am fit as a fiddle now!

P.P.S. Elisabeth asked to be removed from this footnote because it "seems like a lot to put me in the text twice." Bah!

First, Lewis and I tour the pet area. Second, pitching sideways and still attired in my attractive set of Uniqlo long underwear, I stagger to the front desk and announce that I am staying another day. The Hardwick Inn and Suites breakfast room is third. Teetering along, swaying against the people in front of me in line, I rustle up Lewis's two egg patties and bagel, and as I turn, I see her. Ladies! It is Our Heroine of the Waffle Machine! Australian bush hat, godlike calves, stacks of waffles! I return to the room, my faith in womankind renewed, fall happily back in bed, and do not move for another twelve hours.

However difficult it was to get out of that Florence, Alabama, Hardwick Inn and Suites hotel bed, it was more difficult to watch Roger turn into **#16** on **The Most Hideous Men of My Life List.** His Fox News poisoned the country with racist hysteria, divided America with its Festival of Hate & Idiocy, and so by the time Gretchen Carlson, Megyn Kelly, Laurie Dhue, Julie Roginsky, Andrea Tantaros, Rudi Bakhtiar, Laurie Luhn, Kellie Boyle,

Marsha Callahan, and Shelley Ross came forward to tell their
horrible and sometimes violent stories of Roger sexually harassing them, I could peacefully remember that I, E. Jean Carroll,
high-jumper and advice columnist, harassed Roger Ailes *every
single day I had a chance.*

I would harass Roger in the hallway, asking him to twirl so I
could see his behind. I would harass Roger outside the control
room, screeching, "Roger! Make a muscle!" And Roger, unable
to resist, would grab his right wrist with his left hand and perform Body Building Pose Three: Side Chest.

I would harass Roger on live TV, by writing his name (before
the show) on my white knee socks in large black letters. On the
right knee sock:

R
O
G
E
R

On left:

A
I
L
E
S

Then halfway through the show, when talking to a guest, or
answering a caller, I would face the camera and slowly, *slowly* pull
up my trouser legs for the reveal. I would harass Roger when I
was giving interviews to reporters by referring to him as "the
pearl of his sex," and so on. After Gretchen Carlson won $20

million from Fox News to settle her lawsuit, and Roger—in an almost *unthinkable* event—was ousted from Fox, he coached Donald Trump to the presidency. In 2017, he slipped and fell in his $30 million Florida house and died.

Yes, I should probably give myself *another* spot on the **Hideous Men List** for harassing Roger. But weirdly, I thought of it as friends teasing one another, as high jinks, as frolics, as jokes. When Roger married Beth Tilson in a very chic, private ceremony, with Rudolph Giuliani officiating, the wedding video shows me running around shouting to the guests, making toasts, and telling everyone not to worry, that "Roger is *still* my future husband!"

I don't know. Perhaps I was picking up some dark undercurrent in Roger and was inflicting upon him what he would later inflict upon the women at Fox. But that's a guess, and it's probably wrong. The fact is this: no one, not even Donald Trump, has done more to smash America to pieces.* So instead of more guessing, I will recommend Alexis Bloom's stunning *Divide and Conquer: The Story of Roger Ailes* as one of the best documentaries of the decade. And, yes, I tell my story in it.

Ladies, I like Kentucky for five reasons. The cocks crow at high noon. The mountains look like upside-down ice cream cones. One does not wake up in Kentucky motel rooms unable to

---

* And if you don't realize it was Roger Ailes who put Trump in the White House, I love you, but wake up!

move. Kentucky girls don't win beauty pageants by claiming they would like to meet Helen Keller.* And you can change a Kentucky woman's mind. *Viz:*

"Where am I, Miss Jordan Cooper?"

"You're in Bonnieville, Kentucky."

"Where does the name *Bonnieville* come from?"

"I don't know."

"How is that possible?"

"I'm not sure, and I've lived my whole life here too!"

"You were born here?"

"Yes!"

She pulls on her right ear. She is wearing cheery red nail polish.

"Went to school here?"

"Yes."

"Get your mail here?"

"Yes."

Smiling, giggling, large-bosomed, blond braid swishing, Miss Jordan is a belle in the cowgirl mode and staunchly believes that men should run things. On workdays, she is a server at Bob Evans restaurant. At home this morning, she is a bon vivant

---

* Each year, Miss Purdue University, Miss Butler University, Miss Indiana University, Miss Ball State University, etc., etc., compete in the Miss Indiana Pageant. (Ha! Just when you think you've heard the *last* of the frickin' beauty contests, Ladies, *I pull you back in!*)

The question for the five finalists in 1963 was: "What living person would you most like to meet?"

My answer: "Comedy is more important to the world than tragedy, so I'd like to meet Bob Hope." The winner's answer: "Helen Keller." Now, Ladies, Helen Keller was born just outside of Florence, Alabama. I took a photo of the very water pump where blind and deaf Helen learned her first word, *water,* and sent it to the winner, Miss Butler University, who, judging from her Facebook page, still looks quite, *quite* pulchritudinous.

I see I have cut the Helen Keller quote at the opening of this chapter to shreds. Here is what Miss Keller said: "Opportunity is a capricious lady who knocks at every door but once, and if the door isn't opened quickly, she passes on never to return. And that is as it should be. Lovely, desirable ladies won't wait, you have to go out and grab 'em."

wearing a camouflage T- shirt, jeans, and cowgirl boots. Her sunglasses are as big as hot plates.

"I live in the state of New York," I say, "and I've never been to the Statue of Liberty. So we're even."

Miss Jordan bursts into happy laughter.

"How many dogs do you have?" I ask.

We are standing in Miss Jordan's front yard.

"We have seven."

"An excellent number of dogs," I say.

"My mom and my dad do canine search and rescue. They have six."

"*He's* a rescue."

I point to Lewis, who is wearing his ruff of many-colored ribbons and staring lustily at us from the back seat of Miss Bingley. His window is closed because Miss Jordan's cock is crowing. Or perhaps it's Miss Jordan's boyfriend's cock. Or Miss Jordan's neighbor's cock. Whosever cock it is, Lewis wants it for lunch.

"So What Do We Need Men For, Miss Jordan?"

She expels a gust of surprised air.

"[Softly whispering.] That's a tough question."

She smiles.

"I mean, my boyfriend—" Her hand flutters to her chest. "I need him a lot. I really do."

She looks at me, tilting her head in delicate consternation.

"I don't know," she says.

"Now seriously, Miss Jordan. What do you *need* a man for?"

Miss Jordan pushes out her lips, draws them back in, and rolls them up toward her nose.

"[Softly.] Well, I'm not sure."

"Anything?"

"Yeah, well, I'm sure there are lots of things."

"Like . . ."

"Uuuuuuueeee . . ."

Miss Jordan looks off into space for half a minute and then cries:

"I love my boyfriend a lot for working on cars!"

Miss Jordan Cooper of Bonnieville, Kentucky, changes her mind.

Bonnieville is the ruralest of rural hamlets. The little burg of 255 souls, with its working-class houses, chicken coops, dog runs, and a restaurant named Ole Millie's is gently spread across hill and dale, and I am happy to say, Ladies, that there are more cars to be fixed in Miss Jordan's yard than any other.

"What else do you need men for, Miss Jordan?"

Miss Jordan rolls her creamy, pinkish-red lips down and then up and over toward her right ear. She says nothing.

"You're not needy, are you?" I say.

"Yes. I am."

"So you need men for . . . ?"

Again! Stumped! Her lips curl down in a tragedy mask.

"I'm not *suuuurrrrre.*"

I think she looks into my eyes, but I can't tell on account of the sunglasses and the grapefruit-pink streaks of light shooting off into infinity.

A moment passes.

"Humph," says Miss Jordan, disappointed with herself.

"So fixing cars," I say, and I mean it to sting.

"*Wel-llllll* . . . he's my best friend," says Miss Jordan.

"And he's handsome," I say.

It is difficult to judge a man by Kentucky standards, of course, but, Ladies, he is a big, meaty, pleasant chap who fled into the house when I pulled into the driveway.

"He gets a lot of looks," says Miss Jordan. "So companionship. That would be the biggest thing."

"Can you picture a world run by women?"

"[Absolutely definite.] No."

"No?"

"I just . . . No. No. No, I couldn't."

Her lips bang over near her right ear.

"You can't *picture* it?"

"No."

"Just too difficult to imagine?"

"Yeah. I don't know. As for myself, my emotions get in the way too much. I guess a woman's motherly instincts go into effect, you know."

"So . . . you think women are too emotional to run things? Too motherly? Less rational than men?"

"[Wincing.] No."

"But women shouldn't take over?"

"No."

"Many women can't *wait* to run this country, ya know."

"[Taking a stand.] A lot of us around here are still old-fashioned."

"What's your boyfriend doing?"

"He's inside."

"Would you please go get him? I want to know if the men around here are beating the women into submission."

"I'll go get him."

"I need to study this," I say.

She turns, walks across the mottled Kentucky bluegrass, mounts the stairs, and enters the house. I look at the lawn care equipment on the porch and listen to the cock crowing and wonder if I shouldn't tie a hay baler onto the back of Miss Bingley. YES! A big green-and-yellow John Deere hay baler, and as we go along, I just bale up the men we meet and put them all in a big pen.

Because I'm beginning to think it would be easier to get rid of men than to trust women to want to seize power and run things. It seems many women are more likely to use their brains to rationalize men always being in charge than to use their brains to figure out how to take over. We've endured five thousand generations of male whackos running things and we are just *now* starting to stand up for ourselves? No, Ladies. I'm not sure we can trust 100 percent of America's females. I think my way is best. I think I should hook up the hay baler.

Miss Jordan comes out of the house, alone, her hot-plate glasses flashing.

"You can't make him come out?"

"No. No. I couldn't."

"Did he tell you why he likes an old-fashioned girl?"

"[Blushing.] No."

"So were you raised to be an old-fashioned girl?"

"My mother was an RN. She worked nights. My dad worked days. I was raised by my grandparents to be old-fashioned. We all ate dinner together every night. I volunteered at the adult day care. It was a very respectful upbringing."

"So you were brought up to do what men told you to do?"

"No! My mom is very headstrong and very independent. She and my father divorced and then got back together. So, no. I don't think I was raised like that."

"Were you a cheerleader?"

"In elementary school."

"Name five women you'd like to see run the country."

"[Shaking her head.] Nooooooooooo."

"Can you name one?"

"I don't know."

"Please," I say.

"[Laughing.] There's so much in the world you can't do anything about!"

"So maybe women would do a better job," I say.

Her hot plates blaze. "Possibly."

My heart leaps. "A possibility! So contemplate this, Miss Jordan: women take over the country for a couple of years. Do you think things would be better?"

"[Smiling.] Possibly. Maybe."

"How can it be worse?"

"That's true," she says. "We have all this horrible *hate* in the United States. Can't we just stop it?"

"So you're willing to give women a chance to see what they can do?"

She looks down at her mushroom-colored cowgirl boots.

"Well . . . " she says.

The glasses whang out a beam as she looks up.

"I would, yeah."

"You'd be willing to give women a couple of years? Perhaps help them out?"

"I would."

"They might improve things?" I ask.

"They might! You could get some wonderful person up there who would lead! It takes just one person. There may be that one badass woman who could do it! You never know."

And that is how a Kentucky woman changes her mind.

X

"Just Cuz You Have Boobs Doesn't Mean You're Not Strong!"

Elizabethtown, Kentucky
(#27 Most Popular Girl's Name)

Marysville, Ohio
(#160 Most Popular Girl's Name)

Elyria, Ohio
(#13,250 Most Popular Girl's Name)

Seneca Falls, New York
(Not a woman-named town, but as it is the site of the 1848 Women's Rights Convention—the first in the history of the planet—I figure what the hell.)

It is a melancholy object to be pondering the question What Do We Need Men For and at the same time to be driving Miss Bingley up the middle of this great country—Kentucky! Ohio! O, my America!—and *still* see in the streets hundreds of members of the male sex sending dick pics, wondering where the clitoris is, cheating on their wives, taking up two seats, interrupting, lying, stalking, robbing, rioting, murdering, perjuring, passing laws, etc.

So before we finally and forever answer the question What Do We Need Men For, Ladies, let us consider the last-minute details:

If We Decide to Get Rid of Men, Who's Gonna Run Things When They're Gone?

—Name me five women you'd like to see run the country.
  —Mm.
  —Just five women.
  —Uhhhh.
  —Just five.
  —Huhhhhhhh.
  —You live in Marysville, Ohio, right, Miss Sara?
  —Right.
  —So, just name five women who would be a better president

than Warren G. Harding, who is buried in a mausoleum just down the road in Marion.

—Uhhhh.

—OK. Name *any* woman better than Warren G. Harding.

—Kennedy's wife!

—Jackie Kennedy?

—Yeah.

—But she's dead.

—Yeah.

—Good point! Even dead, Jackie Kennedy *would* be a better president than Warren G. Harding. Keep going! You've got a good start! Just four more women. Try to think of women who are actually alive and would be good at running the country.

—I don't know.

—Come on, Sara! Come on! Come on! Jackie Kennedy and . . . you can do it!

—Uh. No one's coming to me.

Sara Barker of Marysville.

You think Sara is the most intellectually negligible woman I can find?

Ha! Sara, the twenty-five-year-old manager of Boston's Restaurant & Sports Bar in Marysville, Ohio, is one of the brightest. I am truly startled to report that *most* women I talk with can't "name five women you'd like to see running the country."

I know this fact is difficult to digest, but just try wading into a flock of seven post-debs in Elizabethtown, Kentucky, who are standing in front of the athletic store, Running Soles, sneering at your kilt and whispering aspersions about your dog probably "not having all his shots."

"Ladies!" I cry. "Can you name five women you'd like to see running the country?"

They are expecting me to say something weird, of course, but for a moment, they still look at me surprised, like Gwyneth Paltrow staring at a jade egg that has run away from its yoni.

"We can give you more than five," says a woman with a lovely smug nose like Madame du Barry.

"Excellent!" I say.

[Silence.]

"Good! Good!" I say. "Yay."

[Silence.]

[Silence.]

"Condi Rice."

"Good!"

[Silence.]

[Silence.]

[Silence.]

[Silence.]

[Silence.]

"You know that brunette on Fox News?" says a very tan woman in running shorts. "She'd be good."

"They're *all* brunette now," I say. "The smart women, i.e., the blondes, are gone."*

[Angry silence.]

[Angry silence.]

[Angry silence.]

"Why can't I think of her name?" says Running Shorts.

[Silence.]

[Silence.]

[Silence.]

[Silence.]

[Silence.]

[Silence.]

[Silence.]

[Silence.]

[Silence.]

[Silence.]

[Silence.]

[Silence.]

[Silence.]

I can say this to the credit of the Elizabethtown Seven. They rustle up Condoleezza Rice in under forty seconds. But the six Men of Marianna—remember them, Ladies? We wanted to sic

---

* Exaggerated, *of course*, BUT . . . with some suing Roger Ailes or Fox News for sexual harassment, others simply leaving or finding their contracts not renewed, Gretchen Carlson, Megyn Kelly, Laurie Dhue (even Greta Van Susteren had turned caramel-blond)—all were gone when I met the Elizabethtown debs.

Carla on them?—the Men of Marianna also come up with Condoleezza Rice, plus Carly Fiorina, Meg Whitman, Senator Susan Collins, and Ambassador Nikki Haley, and they do it in about two and a half minutes.

Miss Sara Barker in Marysville, Ohio, requires eleven minutes to come up with the following five:

Jackie Kennedy
Oprah
Michelle Obama
Ivanka Trump
J. K. Rowling

One is dead, one is a menace to society, one is British, but hey! Sara does better than the seven manic pixie dream girls of *Elizabethtown*.

But the most photogenic list comes from three Indiana women I run into at the Helen Keller home in Florence, Alabama. They are so wise and articulate about political systems, I expect them to reel off a dozen female senators, governors, mayors, CEOs, secretaries of state, etc., etc. Here are the five women they'd like to see running the country:

Oprah
Ellen
Katie Couric
Jane Pauley
Elizabeth Warren

Time: twenty-six seconds. When I ask who their five greatest women actors are (to check if they are a traveling trio of idiot savants going to towns named after women, listing famous chicks with their own TV shows), they draw a complete blank.

Judge Jeanine Pirro turns out to be the woman Running

Shorts was thinking of. Most of the Seven don't stick it out long enough to be edified.

Here is my theory as to why it's difficult for many women to think of female leaders. I have made it into a poem:

> **Women did not create America's**
> **political system.**
> **Men did.**
> **If women get a chance to invent**
> **a new way of governing—**
> **which, of course, we will,**
> **and it will be infinitely superior—**
> **we won't have to rack our brains**
> **envisioning**
> **women leaders.**
> **Because our leaders will be women.**

What women *can* envision right now—without the slightest hesitation—is getting rid of men. For instance, at the National Women's Hall of Fame in Seneca Falls, New York, just to jump ahead in our story, Jennifer and Irene, who both work at the Hall of Fame, suggest that "the men" could be "put out on the golf course," where they can "hit their balls."

The National Women's Hall of Fame, by the by, is hung with photos, bios, and plaques of famous women.

"While I'm here," I say, "I would like to nominate Melania

Trump and put her up there on your wall of fame with Harriet Tubman, Louisa May Alcott, Susan B. Anthony, Maya Angelou, Lucille Ball, Margaret Bourke-White, and Julia Child."

"Go ahead!" says Irene.

"If any woman deserves a plaque on your wall," I say, "it's Melanija Knavs Trump!"

"It's a hundred dollars for the plaque," says Irene, "which we will send to Mrs. Trump. Plus five dollars for the shipping and handling. And then we will display a copy of her plaque on the wall forever."

I pay without trifling and send the plaque to 1600 Pennsylvania Avenue, Washington, D.C. I want it engraved with the following, if possible:

> FOR IDIOCIES SUFFERED AS A RESULT
> OF BEING DONALD TRUMP'S FIRST LADY

I haven't checked, but I believe the permanent copy of the plaque now resides on the wall of the National Women's Hall of Fame. Congratulations, Melania!

Miss Irene and Miss Jennifer at the National Women's Hall of Fame in Seneca Falls, New York, holding my Melania Trump nomination.

It is a bright, clear, dazzling What Do We Need Men For day. Lewis and I are in peak form, waving at the citizens of Elyria, Ohio, playing Aretha as loud as she will go—and Aretha will go very, *very* loud—and heading off over the eight miles to Oberlin, where I set out my FREE ADVICE signs and a big picture of the Ask E. Jean column. After eating the chocolate off a Baby Ruth and giving Lewis the nougat, I sit down on a tree stump in the deep green of Oberlin College and wait to solve my problem.

"Oh, I'm not *offering* advice," I say when two students stop and inquire. "I *need* advice."

"What's your problem?" says the redhead in the pretty navy dress, the gold nose ring, and the black yarmulke pinned to the back of her head.

Yes! I say, *her* head, *her her her.*

Oh, I *know* this is Oberlin College, vanguard of gay, lesbian, bisexual, transgender, and queer rights, alma mater of Lena "I-haven't-had-an-abortion-but-I-wish-I-had" Dunham,* and I know the tall redhead was probably born a boy, but I ignore Oberlin custom, break the laws of God and genderqueers, and do not ask—repeat, do *not* ask—the two students to tell me their preferred pronouns. No. I simply address them, quite seriously, as the Future of All Womanhood.

"*We-e-e-e-elll,*" I say, "my problem is that all the problems coming into the Ask E. Jean column are caused by men."

---

* Ladies, you get that Miss Lena is joking, right?

"All the problems in the world *are* caused by cis men," says the second student, a very small, very comely, very built young person with shoulders like reinforced concrete, a face like a Vargas pinup girl, a breathtaking chestnut ponytail, strong little thighs bursting out of cut-off jeans, biceps bursting out of a little striped T-shirt, and a glad smile exploding on her face. She turns out to be a powerlifter majoring in neuroscience named Zooey.

"So," I say, "I'm beginning to think we don't need men."

The redhead, Diane, pale as a Botticelli and splashed all over with vermilion freckles, pulls a coil of her russet hair out as far as it will go—which is about a foot.

"Realistically," she says, "we *don't* need men for anything."

"But, Miss Diane," I say. (Yes! Absolutely! *Miss*!) "Can women create a political system without men?"

"Oh, I think we could figure it out," she says.

"It may shock you," says Zooey, lowering the outside edges of her eyebrows like Gene Tierney—an involuntary motion, wonderfully winning and endearing—"but women can do anything men can do."

"And we can do it faster and less distracted," says Diane.

"Big talk," I say.

"I don't need to go into powerlifting, *do I?*" says Zooey, taking Lewis's leash out of my hand so I can shoot a better video of our chat with my iPhone. "The current all-gender records are held by a woman, Kim Wolford—last night, she broke her own record and deadlifted 523 pounds. Just cuz you have boobs doesn't mean you're not strong!"

Lewis looks up at Zooey with a rapt gleam in his eyes, and, after considering, he offers her his paw, and to his delirious surprise, Zoey squats down on her haunches and puts her arms around him.

"So how would the country look if women ran it?" I say.

Diane pulls a coil of hair from the back of her head and ponders.

"Well, the idea of spending billions of dollars to blow up

other countries! It is so stupid! So manic! If women ran the
United States, it would not apply."

She lets go of the coil of hair, and it springs back with such
fury, I am surprised it doesn't knock her over.

"And our gun problem wouldn't *be* a problem," says Zooey,
with Lewis swooning under her pattings and pettings.

"And I would warrant," says Diane—*I would warrant*—Diane
talks like a character straight out of *Middlemarch*—"that sexual harassment at work would be cut down to a fraction, a *small* fraction!"

"You're an English major, Miss Diane?" I say.

"Religious studies and math."

"Ah! Really? Is there a statue of Antoinette Brown on campus?"

"Who?"

"Antoinette Brown."

They chew on the name, first staring at one another, then
staring at me.

"The first woman in the United States," I say, "to become an
ordained minister."

If they are thrilled with this information, they are even more
thrilled when I add:

"She graduated from Oberlin."

It is being thrilled like this that will probably get them so
disliked when they enter the job market—but persevere, Future
of All Womanhood!

"You have to see the monument for Adelia Field Johnson,
who was the first female professor!" says Zooey excitedly.

"A statue of a woman?" I say. "A *woman*? Really?!"

"It's actually not a statue," says Zooey. "It's a plaque."

"I knew it!" I scream. "*Goddamned fucking plaques!*"

One doesn't want to upset the young scholars, and Lewis is
lifting his head to rebuke me for disturbing his love-in with
Zooey, but come *on*. "They erect thousands of statues to men
and give women fucking plaques!" I cry.

Diane replies sublimely:

"I guess women lack that male insecurity that causes men to build statues of themselves."

"So if women are gonna run things," I say, "what do we do with the men?"

"I'm a big fan of camp," says Diane.

"Yes!" I say. "Camp! We'll put saltpeter into their mashed potatoes!"

"And," says Diane, "if a few dozen of them misbehave, well—*crrrrrrrrrreeeeeeek*—she draws her finger across her throat—we'll take out a few as an example."

Zooey jumps to her feet.

"We have to go," she says, handing Lewis's leash to me. "We have an appointment." And with that, she seizes Diane's arm, turns her about, and they run—literally run—away. Lewis barks and barks for Zooey to come back, but the Future of All Womanhood disappears into the dark green glades of Oberlin.

The following is a small selection of responses from your advice columnist's unscientific, nonobjective, and totally prejudiced survey on Facebook:

If We Decide to Get Rid of Men, Where Will We Put Them?

A biodome
With the secret tribes in the Amazon
Day care

Container ships
In therapy
The planet Jupiter
A cigar lounge
Lysistrata-ville
A blender
In a room with their mothers
On that island where Wonder Woman came from
In a galaxy far, far away
A medically induced coma
That cave where the Thai footballers got trapped
Mar-a-Lago

A trinity of males I would like sent to any or *all* of the above places are: **A)** an idiot who blew his fuse and tried to pound me into rape-able submission; **B)** a moron who refused to give me a passport unless I had dinner with him and sat on his lap; and **C)** a fur trapper in Montana, whose traps I sprayed daily with Lysol (and who was too stupid to figure out why he never caught and crushed the legs of beautiful wild foxes and therefore could not sell their hides to unpleasant people who make fur coats for thoughtless morons to wear). In other words, **#17** a network publicist—not from CBS—who attacked me in his car the *same* week Moonves attacked me in the Nikko Hotel elevator, **#18** a South African Diplomat, and **#19** a torturer of animals. All make E. Jean's Parade of Assholes, or as it is known, **The Most Hideous Men of My Life List.**

And whattya know, here come Diane and Zooey skipping and spinning back to me through the green gloaming.

"We googled you!" shouts Zooey, receiving Lewis's nose up her shorts—his extra-special greeting.

"We must apologize!" says Diane.

"We thought you were one of those people who were going to take us out of context!" says Zooey.

"And make us look bad!" says Diane.

"But it turns out that you're E. Jean Carroll! Ha! Ha! Ha! Ha! Ha! Ha! Ha! Ha! Ha! Ha! Ha! Ha!"

This fact strikes them as so funny they both practically collapse on the Oberlin grass.

"I'll tell you what," I say. "I'll change your names in the book. Would you like that?"

"We get new names?"

"Totally new."

"Any name we want?"

"Any."

"Can I be Diane?"

"You will be Diane."

"I can't think of one," says Zooey.

"Take any name!" I say.

"All I can think of," she says, "is Salinger's *Franny and Zooey.* And I can't be called Franny."

Ladies, Melania Trump or no Melania Trump, I am sick of this plaque business. I, therefore, propose that we erect a statue to every woman in America over the age of twenty-five, and I would like each of you to choose a moment in your life that you would like to commemorate.

For example, a seven-foot monument of bronze-like material memorializing the day you scored the winning goal for your hockey team would capture you in shoulder pads, shin guards, helmet, and skates, your arms raised in triumph.

I will use a 3-D printer to make it.

3-D printers are excellent at printing guns. Why not print seven-foot-tall statues of women? We will erect them in front of every residence in America containing a woman age 25–117. So, Ladies, start thinking how you would like to be immortalized. I am already drawing up plans and testing marble-like substances. Send a note with photo to E.Jean@AskEJean.com . I'll put it on ejeancarroll.com to be hailed with universal delight.

XI

"Go Try This On."

Angelica, New York
(#755 Most Popular Girl's Name)

1 ⋯⋯▶

Ladies, are you good at buying gifts?

2 ⋯⋯▶

Lisa Birnbach went to Thailand and Cambodia, and brought me home a small china elephant. It was wearing ruby toenail polish and a fringed headdress with gold tassels.

"Oh!" I cried, looking into the little elephant's sweet brown eyes. "I love her! I'll call her Elsbeth! She'll bring me luck!" Two days later, I fell off a bridge on the Appalachian Trail and broke my arm in four places.

After my arm was set at the hospital, I came home, seized Elsbeth by her little trunk, and hurled her into the garbage can with the pet lock.

So I owe Lisa Birnbach a present from the What Do We Need Men For trip. Angelica, an eccentric little village in the foothills of New York's leg of the Appalachian Mountains, looks like a good place to buy it.

I leave Lewis Carroll in the car and am walking in the direction of a shop called Two Doors Down and here comes a plump young woman with blond-gold hair and blond eyebrows strolling along Angelica's main street with a little girl.

"What Do We Need Men For?" I ask.

She stops and lights a cigarette.

"Well . . . " she says.

Scarlet leaves are falling, blackberry pies are baking, the place absolutely crawls with quaintness.

"We must need men for *something*," I say.

"I just had a baby," says the young woman. "I guess I needed a man for *that*."

"Oh! A little sister or brother for you!" I say to the little girl who has long blond ringlets and is jumping back and forth over a crack in the sidewalk.

She looks up at me like I am something that has just crawled down from a tree.

"It's my cousin!" says the little girl.

"Ah!"

"This is my niece," says the young woman.

"A cousin is twice as good!" I say.

"Yes!"

"So what else do we need men for?" I say.

"Let me think," says the young woman with the cigarette.

"OK," I say. "I'll catch up with you."

I cross the street.

"I've never seen shoes like those," says a chap in a yellow field coat, pointing to my three-toned saddle shoes. He is sitting at a square black wrought-iron table outside the Angelica Sweet Shop with two friends.

I take off my right shoe and hand it to him.

"It's beast-free, floatable, shock-absorbing, waterproof, odor-killing, foam-injected molded EVA, comes in 999 colors, and is certified by PETA," I say.

He takes off *his* shoe.

Angelica, New York, is named for the famous eighteenth-century wit and clotheshorse Angelica Schuyler, whose beauty and courage were so great that she could marry one man and be in love with another. Renée Elise Goldsberry won the 2016 Tony Award when she played Angelica, the secret lover of Alexander Hamilton, in *Hamilton,* the musical by Lin-Manuel Miranda. And as *Hamilton* also won ten other Tonys, principally *costume* (i.e., shoes), I would be surprised if footwear was *not* a constant topic in Angelica, and the fellow and I enjoy a bracing conversation about cap toes, lace-ups, master last-makers, rare leathers, etc., etc.

The man's two friends, a mild, smiling, agreeable chap in a navy blue windbreaker—a retired physicist—and his wife, a demure, friendly woman in a buttoned-up blue cotton cardigan, running shoes with lime-green laces, and hair that shade of pewter some women look so attractive wearing in the final quarter of their lives, nod in a golden mist of affability.

Before I duck into the Angelica Sweet Shop for some blackberry pie, I say civilly:

"What Do We Need Men For?"

The woman with the pewter hair swells up about fifteen times her size.

"Women do too much complaining!" she shouts.

I am tickled to death!

"Nah, women don't complain enough," I say, laughing. "We need to complain more."

"No! No!" cries the woman.

Her dazzlingly blue eyes grow bluer.

"*Sooo,*" I say, "you believe we need—"

"Professors in colleges!" she shouts. "*Professors!* Professors are stirring up our young women so badly that I once held a door for a young woman and she called me a name!"

"What was it?" I say, fascinated.

I glance at her husband.

"We've learned to get along," he says, smiling.

"They go everywhere together," says the shoe aficionado.

"*What are women complaining about?*" the woman shouts. "I want to know!"

"Well, they are complaining about not making—"

She cuts me off.

"This is a wonderful country! It gives women so much! I am from Germany. My sister still lives in Germany, and she writes to me and asks, 'Why are the women marching? Why are they wearing those hats?' I tell her they are wearing the hats because they are being stirred up by the professors and the fake media! Fake news! I mean, what *is* there to complain about?"

I am so stunned by her passion and so overwhelmed with the strain of a confrontation—which, due to my mother, as we all know, Ladies, I would chew off my left arm to avoid—that I pause a split second, choosing among the zillion complaints—women earning 84 percent of what men earn . . . 81 percent of women experiencing sexual harassment . . . only 5 percent of Fortune 500 companies being run by women, etc.—and, of course, the pause is fatal. Because *BOOM!* Off she goes:

"And don't tell me about Hillary!" she shouts.

"A great woman," I say.

"Hillary was LaLaLaLaLa after Benghazi!" screams the woman. "Hillary should be locked up!"

Ladies, are you good at advising *other* people what gifts to buy?

Before we begin, the two great handicaps to telling you what happened to me in Bergdorf's are: **A)** the man I will be talking about—not to mention his team, his lawyers, his party, his friends on Fox News, etc.—will deny it—as he has denied accusations of sexual misconduct made by at least sixteen credible women, namely, Jessica Leeds, Kristin Anderson, Jill Harth, Cathy Heller, Temple Taggart McDowell, Karena Virginia, Bridget Sullivan, Tasha Dixon, Mindy McGillivray, Rachel Crooks, Natasha Stoynoff, Jennifer Murphy, Jessica Drake, Ninni Laaksonen, Summer Zervos, and Cassandra Searles; and **B)** I run the risk of making him *more* popular by revealing what he did.

His admirers can't get enough of hearing that he's rich enough, lusty enough, and powerful enough to be sued by and to pay off every splashy porn star or *Playboy* Playmate who "comes forward," so I can't imagine how ecstatic the poor saps will be to hear their favorite Walking Phallus got it on with an old lady in the world's most prestigious department store.

There are several facts, however—and I will try to make them as unsexy as possible so as to not turn up the gonadal glow of his base—facts that are so odd that I want to clear them up now before we start:

Did I report the attack to the police?
No.

Did I tell anyone about the attack?
Yes. I told two close friends. The first friend, a journalist, writer for *New York* and *Vanity Fair* magazines, correspondent on the TV morning shows, author of eight books, etc., begged me to go to the police the night it happened.

"He raped you," she kept repeating when I called her. "He raped you. Go to the police! I'll go with you. We'll go together." She also said several times: "E. Jean, I don't think this is funny," because—and this is one of the strangest facts of all—I could not stop laughing.

My second friend was also a journalist, a New York anchorperson, whom I saw almost every day at work when I was doing the daily *Ask E. Jean* show on America's Talking and the *Wrap Up* with Steve Doocy (a highlight show featuring clips from America's Talking, which Roger Ailes ran on the weekends on CNBC). My friend grew very quiet when I told her, grasped both my hands in her own, and said, "Tell no one. Forget it! He has two hundred lawyers. He'll *bury* you."

Do I have photos or any visual evidence?
Bergdorf's security cameras must have picked us up at the

Fifty-eighth Street entrance of the store. We would have been filmed on the ground floor in the bags and hats sections. Cameras also must have captured us going up the escalator, walking toward the lingerie department, and no doubt, within the lingerie department. I'm not certain, but I think New York law at the time permitted security cameras in dressing rooms of department stores to "prevent theft." The attack occurred almost twenty-four years ago. If it was captured on tape, depending on the position of the camera, it would be very difficult to see the man unzipping his pants because he was wearing a topcoat. The struggle might simply have appeared as "sexy." During the mid-'90s, before all data was stored in the cloud, even a most painstakingly judicious company like Bergdorf Goodman probably erased the tapes after ninety days. But, maybe, perhaps by some miracle, they have the evidence of the attack collected somewhere.

Do I have DNA evidence?
I don't know. I do not believe the man ejaculated. However, I never dry-cleaned the Donna Karan coatdress. It's still hanging on the back of the door in my closet.

Why were there no sales attendants in the lingerie department?
Bergdorf Goodman's perfections are so well known, it is a store so noble, so gracious, so clubby, so posh, that it is almost easier to accept the fact that I was attacked than the fact that, for a very brief period, there was no sales attendant in the lingerie department. *Inconceivable* is the word. Sometimes a person won't find a sales attendant in Saks—it's true—sometimes one has to look for a sales associate in Barneys, Bloomingdale's, or even Tiffany's; but 99 percent of the time, you will have an attendant in Bergdorf's. All I can say is, I did not—in this fleeting episode—see an attendant. And the other odd thing is that a dressing room door was open. In Bergdorf's dressing room, doors are usually closed and locked until a client wants to try something on.

Why haven't I "come forward" before now?

Receiving death threats, being driven from my home, being dismissed, being dragged through the mud, and joining the sixteen women who've come forward with credible stories about how the man grabbed, badgered, belittled, mauled, molested, and assaulted them only to see the man turn it around, deny, threaten, and attack them doesn't sound like much fun. Also, I'm a coward.

Have I suffered mental anguish, depression, anxiety, RTS (rape trauma syndrome), etc., due to the attack?

Very little. It was a big event in my life, and very frightening, but the incident has left me strangely untouched. I was slightly disordered immediately after, yes. But I've always been blessed with resilience throughout my seven decades, and I only suffer when I think about what unbearable horrors other women may have suffered at his instigation.

In fact, I've continued to shop at Bergdorf's. Recently, I bought a pair of Ted Muehling earrings for Robbie Myers, the editor in chief of *Elle,* when she stepped down after seventeen years of running the magazine, and last week Bergdorf's filled me to the brim with champagne while Lisa Birnbach and I whooped or groaned at my niece Lauren Switzer as she tried on wedding dresses—and the attack never entered my head. Indeed, before 2015, when the man began appearing in the papers and on TV daily, I rarely thought of it. When he forced himself on the notice of the entire nation, I, like everyone else, tweeted jokes about him, complained to friends that America was going to hell in a handbasket, and so on. I am fine. I can't explain it, but I never suffered. If I feel any agony at all, it is when I think that what he did to me in that dressing room is what he is doing today to the country.

So, now I will tell you what happened:

This is during the years I'm doing the daily *Ask E. Jean* TV show, a small hit on the network Roger Ailes starts, called America's Talking, which soon becomes MSNBC.

Bergdorf Goodman, the grand department store, has a side entrance on Fifty-eighth Street, and early one evening, I am going out the revolving door, and one of New York's most famous men is coming *in* the revolving door, or it could have been a regular door at that time, I can't recall, and he says:

"Hey, you're that Advice Lady!"

And I say to **#20** on **The Most Hideous Men of My Life List:**

"Hey, you're that Real Estate Tycoon!"

I am surprised at how good-looking he is. We have met once before and, perhaps it is the early evening light, but he looks prettier than ever. This has to be in the fall of 1995 or the spring of 1996, because he's garbed in a faultless topcoat and I'm wearing my black wool Donna Karan coatdress and high heels, but not a coat. I don't recall that I'm carrying shopping bags, so I must be—I can't remember and am guessing—on my way out the door because I'm heading to Barneys to find whatever I can't get at Bergdorf's.

"Come advise me," says the man. "I gotta buy a present."

"Oh!" I say, charmed. "For whom?"

"A girl," he says.

"Don't the assistants of your secretaries buy things like that?" I say.

"Not this one," he says. Or, perhaps, he says, "Not this time." I can't recall. He is a big talker, and from the instant we collide, he yammers about himself like he's Alexander the Great ready to loot the city of Babylon.

As we are standing just inside the door, I point to the handbags. "How about—"

"No!" he says, making the face where he pulls up both lips like he's balancing a spoon under his nose, and begins talking about how he once thought about buying Bergdorf's.

"Or . . . a hat!" I say, enthusiastically, walking toward the handbags, which, at the period I'm telling you about—and Bergdorf's has been redone two or three times since 1995/96—are mixed in with, and displayed next to, the hats. "She'll love a hat! You can't go wrong with a hat!"

I don't remember what he says, but he comes striding along— greeting a Bergdorf sales attendant like he owns the joint and permitting a shopper to gape in awe at him, and goes right for a fur number.

"*Please,*" I say. "No woman would wear a dead animal on her head!"

What he replies I don't recall, but I remember he coddles the fur hat like it's a baby otter.

"How old is the lady in question?" I say.

"How old are you?" says the man, fondling the hat and looking at me like Louis Leakey carbon-dating a thighbone he's found in Olduvai Gorge.

"I'll tell you my age when you show me your tax return," is what I *wish* I had said.

It's *now* the answer I give to men who ask how old my female friends are when I'm fixing them up on blind dates. *So how old am I?* If I have run into this man in the fall of 1995 after my birthday, which is December 12, or in the spring of 1996 (I've tried; I can't pin it down any closer), my reply is:

"Fifty-two."

"You're so *old!*" he says, laughing, and it's at about this point he drops the hat, looks across the store in the direction of the escalator, and says, "Lingerie!" So we stroll to the escalator. I don't remember anybody else greeting him or galloping up to talk to him which indicates how very few people are in the store at the time.

I have no recollection where lingerie is in the '95/'96 Bergdorf's, but it seems to me it is on a floor with the evening gowns and bathing suits, and when the man and I arrive—and my memory now is vivid—no one is present.

There are two or three dainty boxes and a lacy, see-through bodysuit of lilac gray on the counter. The man snatches the bodysuit up and says:

"Go try this on!"

"*You* try it on," I say, laughing. "It's *your* color."

"Try it on, come *on,*" he says, throwing it at me.

"It goes with your eyes," I say, laughing and throwing it back.

"You're in good shape," he says, holding the filmy thing up against me. "I wanna see how this looks."

"But it's *your* size," I say, laughing and trying to slap him back with one of the boxes on the counter.

"Come on," he says, taking my arm. "Let's put this on."

"This is gonna be hilarious," I'm saying to myself—and as I write this, I am staggered by my stupidity. As we head to the dressing rooms, I'm laughing aloud and saying in my mind: *I'm gonna make him put this thing on over his pants!*

The moment the dressing room door is closed, he lunges at me, pushes me against the wall, bumping my head quite badly, and puts his mouth against my lips. I am so shocked, I shove him back and start laughing again. He seizes both my arms and pushes me up against the wall a second time, bumping my head, and, as I become aware of how large he is, he holds me against the wall with his shoulder and jams his hand under my coatdress and pulls down my tights.

I am astonished by what I'm about to write: I keep laughing.

The next moment, still wearing correct business attire, shirt, tie, suit jacket, overcoat, he opens the overcoat, unzips his pants, and, forcing his fingers around my private area, then thrusts his penis halfway—or completely, I'm not certain—inside me. It turns into a colossal struggle. I am too frightened to panic. I am wearing a pair of sturdy, black patent-leather, four-inch Barneys high heels. I try to stomp his foot. I try to push him off with my one free hand—for some reason I keep holding my purse with the other—and I finally get a knee up high enough to push him out and off, and I turn, open the door, and run out of the dressing room.

The whole episode lasts no more than two or three minutes. I don't remember if any person or attendant is now in the lingerie department. I don't remember if I run for the elevator or if I take the slow ride down on the escalator. As soon as I land on the main floor, I run through the store and out the door—I don't recall which door—and find myself outside on Fifth Avenue. And that's it. I've never had sex with anybody ever again.

"*So, have you had* time to think?" I say, bumping into the young woman with blond-gold hair in front of the Angelica post office. "What Do We Need Men For?"

"Nothing," she says.

"*Noooooooothinnnnnnng!*" warbles the little girl.

"I like men," says the young woman.

"Oh!" I say. "Men have written great symphonies and painted great pictures. I just don't think they should run everything."

"I like men," says the young woman, "but anything I need them for, I can do myself."

"Can you fix your washing machine?" I ask.

"No. I have to call a man."

"I watched three YouTube videos," I say, "and fixed mine *myself!*"

"See?" says the young woman.

Up comes her chin.

"That's what I mean!" she says. "We don't need 'em!"

P.S. Re: The Garbage Can with Pet Lock: After I tossed Elsbeth in the trash, I started thinking of her shut inside with the discarded cat treat containers, forsaken shredded cheese packages, forlorn bread wrappers, dead Eucerin Intensive Repair jars, etc., etc., with her little trunk raised up, crying, her beautiful headdress of gold tassels being tossed about, and I could not stand it! I retrieved her and put her high up on the top shelf of the bookcase, where she is now quite happy.

P.P.S. Instead of blackberry pie, I bought a pizza to split with Lewis. I forgot to get Lisa's present.

XII

"Let's Do It!"

Eden, Vermont
(#131 Most Popular Girl's Name)

1

Bandanna, earring, shades, leathers, stinking armpits . . . a brute, a monster, a chain-whipping Hun . . . one big muscle of terrifying menace . . . Vermont's version of a Hell's Angel walks from the Eden General Store across Vermont's "Scenic Route 100 Byway," contemplates the FREE ADVICE signs that I have set up on top of Miss Bingley's roof, looks at the dog with the aquamarine hair, stares for a moment at my kilt, and says:

"My wife sent me over."

"No way," I say.

"Yeah."

"Get outta here!" I say.

He points.

Across the highway, to the right of the Eden General Store, on the far side of the gas pumps, beyond the parked trucks, next to a huge Harley, I see a woman with a heap of tawny hair waving at me from the back of a Bark-o-Lounger, a bike so big it practically has a sauna.

"She *sent* you?" I say.

I throw her a wave back.

"She wants to know, 'What advice?'" he says, pointing to my FREE ADVICE signs.

I open an *Elle* magazine and show him the Ask E. Jean column.

"Tell your wife that I am an advice columnist and that if she is having problems with you, to come on over."

"I'll tell her," he says and muscle-walks his giant thighs back across the highway, shoves his big bulk between the trucks, slides up to his wife, and, though I cannot hear—seventy or eighty yards separate us—I watch in astonishment as the colossal chap inclines his head like a male dove cooing to his mate and relays the message.

The woman laughs, looks across at me, and shakes her head. The big man gets on the Harley. The tawny woman kicks up her Bark-o-Lounger. They start their engines, and, before I can cross the highway with Lewis to stop them, they roar away in a burst of glamorous thunder.

Who is this genius woman?

I know that men are only masses of neurological and biological processes, but how did she train her Genghis Khan-on-a-bike to walk across a highway—WALK! Rampaging hordes never walk—in *front* of his fellow men gassing up at the Eden General Store, and do her bidding? I have no idea, but she fills me with confidence and gives me faith that we can pull this off, Ladies!

Lewis and I take up our Free Advice station once again.

A few minutes later, another man appears, not in a car, not on a bike, no, he comes sauntering across the field.

"What kind of mileage are you getting with your Prius?" he asks.

"Forty-seven to fifty-two highway," I say. "Fifty-three town."

"My wife asked me to check," he says. "She's got a Prius. Also, she sent me to tell you that there's a quilting exhibition in Morristown."

What the hell is going on here, Ladies?

Has Miss Bingley catapulted us into another dimension? Do women here have a secret way of ordering men around that no other women possess? Eden is tucked away, it is true, like Shangri-la, high in the mountains of Vermont's Northeast Kingdom, isolated, one of the hidden lands, perhaps one of the seven beyul mentioned in Tibetan scripture; and, you want to know what I think? I think that if this is not a parallel universe, then these chicks are putting something in the water. How else explain two men in a row doing their wives' bidding?

But wait! A third bloke now appears, this time in a lava-gray Honda Civic. He parks, climbs out of the vehicle—shaved skull, overcast eyebrows, rather handsome—says hello to Lewis, and lowering his head as if approaching Catherine the Great, delivers the most stupendous nod at me, a nod that all but throws itself prostrate at my feet and embraces my knees, and says:

"I need a woman's advice."

"Please take a seat, sir," I say, indicating one of the attractive director's chairs I have set out for this very purpose. "Baby Ruth?"

"No, thank you."

"You're in love?" I say.

"How did you know?"

"The joy and terror on your face."

"It's *that* easy to see?" he says, surprised.

"Tell me about her."

"She's a pianist," he says.

"Ah!"

"I have written her a concerto."

"You're a composer!"

"And this piece will *make* her career!"

"Wonderful! I love it! I love it!"

His lips twist into a sad, ironic smile.

"But the men at Carnegie Hall," he says, "won't accept my composition."

You see, Ladies, what have I been telling you? Even *men's* problems are caused by men. Which brings us to **#21** on **The Most Hideous Men of My Life List:** a state governor (male) released a killer (male) on parole, and it was a dog (a bitch) who saved me.

2 ··········▶

Ladies, you are looking at the great Hepburn de Balzac. Not long after this photo was taken—it ran in the first years of "Ask E. Jean" in *Elle* magazine—Hepburn saved me from **#21**, Reginald McFadden, a rapist on what the papers later called a "killing spree."

    I was on the porch of my cottage outside Nyack, New York, filling the bird feeders. The man, a very good-looking man, stopped his car in front of the cottage, got out, and was coming toward me, crossing the yard, saying, "It's nice around here. Any houses for sale?" when Hepburn thudded out on the porch and, without making a sound, lowered her head and let the drool *pour* from her jaws. It was one of the eeriest things I've ever seen—no bark, no growl, she just eyed him as if he were standing rib roast.

The man recoiled, turned, walked swiftly to his car, got in, slammed the door, and sped away. He raped my neighbor later that evening and tried to kill her. The police caught him six or seven days later, and I recognized his picture when it ran in *The New York Times*. He had murdered at least three people and was a "person of interest" in several more. Lewis Carroll wears Hepburn's (resized!) collar in her honor.

Lewis and I meet a Vermont hunting dog the next morning after the Free Advice episode with the doleful composer. It is a foggy, wet What Do We Need Men For day, with air thick as meringue. Lewis and I are rambling around Eden's mountains, and as we wander up a little gorge, we see an orange glow approaching us. A moment later, out of the haze, here come four men with shotguns.

Each chump is upholstered in a thick wool shirt that smells—at eighteen yards' distance—like the men's toilet in a Shell Station. On their heads are identical Day-Glo orange acrylic hats that look like the joke Day-Glo condoms you give a bridegroom at his bachelor party. Over their foul-smelling shirts, each man has tied a hot-orange polyester vest so as to not get shot by other men with hot-orange polyester vests tied over *their* foul-smelling wool shirts. And their bottoms? Wet canvas pants, and if you have ever tried walking up a mountainside in wet canvas pants, Ladies, you know it feels like your pubic grove is being pulled out three hairs at a time.

But here they come up the gorge, the four Blockheads of the Apocalypse, breathing hard, their faces red as boiled tomatoes from falling down ravines chasing tame grouse that have been released (probably that very morning) by the Vermont Fish and Wildlife Department, birds that I could catch with my bare hands and take home for pets. Cowering behind one of the men is a poor confused dog whom they have buckled too tightly into a remote-controlled shock collar.

Lewis and I biff along with them for a chat.

"Gentlemen!" I say. "Good shooting this morning?"

"No," replies one of the Last Words of Nature.

"Too bad!" I say, elated.

And, as I smile at them, I think, *Well, well, well, this is what almighty men have come to, eh? Fat, lardy, pasty, wimpy, out-of-shape, chickenshit pantywaists chasing tame birds through a forest? Well, chumps, maybe you should just give old E. Jean your poor electrocuted dog, and the women of Eden and I will pack you and your hot orange hats off to someplace* special *forever.*

Or, rather . . .

A woman's character mellows when she is on the road.

Hearing, for instance, the plaintive shrieks of the Elizabeth-town Seven enumerating what they need men for—"Support!" "Encouragement!" "Companionship!" "Comfort!"—all traits that can be supplied by a Maine coon cat, but still, Ladies, it gives a jerk to one's heart, does it not? Four thousand miles and a few more incidents of this kind, have, I admit, turned me from an advice columnist of chilled steel into a sensitive woman.

In short, I no longer believe we should fatten up the chaps and sell their elements. No, not even if we could get as much as $1.09 per man! Instead, I propose a new idea, which I hope will meet with your approval, Ladies, and it is this:

We round up all the men and put them in Montana.

Then we'll retrain them.

I have spent many years in Montana, as you know, and I have been assured by a team of female scientists that the erection of an invisible, wireless Man-Containment Fence that encloses the state and extends from Westby (northeast) to the Kootenai National Forest (northwest) down to Yellowstone National Park (southwest) and Belle Creek (southeast) can be completed within eight weeks and will paralyze any human equipped with a penis and/or testicles who tries to cross the boundary.*

I know what you are thinking, Ladies. You are saying to yourself, "But, E. Jean! We can't put the men in Montana because they would seize the 150 Minuteman III intercontinental ballistic missiles at Montana's Malmstrom Air Force Base, and vaporize the female sex off the planet."

Not to worry. The underground Launch Control Center at Malmstrom Air Force Base will be reprogrammed by three female operatives. If any man presses a launch button, a Minuteman III will rise from its silo with its twelve nuclear warheads, shoot three miles above the earth, turn around, head back to where it came from, and explode on the control center.

Men built these things, and they can keep them.

I know you possess warm hearts, Ladies. You fret! You agonize! You doubt that there will enough food and medical care for 119 million men.† But female scientists absolutely guarantee that there will be such an *abundance* of male farmers, doctors, and preachers residing within the Male Containment State that all men will be kept fit, body and soul. Of course, as we will also be emptying the 2,116,759 men currently locked up in state and federal prisons into Montana, there *is* a chance that the men themselves will put an end to the whole male species before the farmers grow their first ears of corn.

---

* At first, I thought we could simply paralyze all humans with large egos, but one of the scientists tells me this would result in freezing as many females as males, including your advice columnist.

† Boys eighteen and under will, of course, *beg* to be sent to Montana because of the whole cowboy thing, but they will remain at home with their mothers to be nurtured into true-blue, stand-up guys.

6

And who will be retraining the men?

Female robots. Yes! Ladies! Robotrixes. Remember I told you about how I lost all my money with **#14,** the celebrated Wall Street Investment Dunce? And remember, just when I thought I would not be able to put food on the table for Lewis, *robots* began making me money on the stock market? And why are robots making me money? *Because they are learning with every trade.* You remember, right?

Well, in a mere five years, our female robots, evolving with every experience, and using my training methods, will turn these chumps, half-wits, scoundrels, jerks, degenerates, jackoffs, dingbats, and creeps into strong, faithful, affable, dependable, trustworthy, kind, intelligent, funny, honest, upright fellows who will quit starting wars and leave all toilet seats down.

Naturally, because our female robots will also be building female robots smarter than they are, and those female robots will be building female robots smarter than *they* are, they will sooner or later become *so* smart they will take over the Earth, and, yes, one day, they will look back at us, Ladies, like we are pubic bones found in Neanderthal caves, but it's a risk I think we should take.

I can't conceive of one objection to this proposal, unless it is urged that wives who are in love with their husbands—and women carrying on torrid affairs with chaps—will be loath to give up their fellows for five years. I have put much thought into this, and I believe that we should set aside Yellowstone National Park for conjugal "tent visits" and permit trysts twice a week (or four times a week for the more hot-blooded females). The tents surrounding Old Faithful geyser will be awarded to the men who show the most improvement.

I am still cogitating the problem of women who, though they will be living in the most delicious and brilliant country in the world—a country run superbly by females—and who will be allowed to do whatever they please, unmolested, unraped, will still be miserable without men. I'm talking about the type of woman who will trample her own mother to get to an asshole.

I'm afraid that these women will fling themselves through the Man-Containment Fence, join the men in Montana, and refuse to budge. These women, I say, are still being cogitated in the old E. Jean brain, but no doubt I will soon come up with an answer for the good of the entire human race.

Or, if I don't come up with an answer, we can simply vote all the chumps *out* of office, vote the women *into* office, and completely take over.

Epilogue

Press Release, Frog Island

Frog Island, New York, November 7, 2017—Advice Columnist, E. Jean Carroll, and her standard poodle, Lewis Carroll, returned from their historic 4,099-mile What Do We Need Men For trip at 3:35 P.M. today. Wearing her Anti-Bird-Killer collar of red, blue, purple, pink, and yellow ribbons, Vagina T. Fireball, the writer's cat, ran across the yard, darted over the bridge, and jumped into Carroll's arms.

"Vagina T., old girl!" cried the writer, burying her face in the animal's fur.

Looking happy but tired, and attired in a kilt of McKinney plaid, with glops of a Dairy Queen sundae down the front, Carroll said the trip was a "huge success."

"For twenty-five years, I have been receiving letters from women complaining about men," she said. "And for twenty-five years, I have been telling them, 'Get rid of the chumps!' But was I right? Or was I wrong? *Should we get rid of men?* I had to hit the road to find out What We Need Men For, before being 100 percent certain."

The advice columnist, her Korean driving cap pulled down at a jaunty angle, stood on the bridge leading to her private Frog Island—a body of land about the size of a Persian carpet—petting Vagina T. as Lewis Carroll, leaping up, nearly knocked the cat into the river.

"It's strange," said the woman known to her many readers as Auntie Eeee, "but when you stop and think about it, I've withstood encounters with Roger Ailes, Les Moonves, and President Trump. I was attacked by a military cadet, molested by a camp counselor, raped by an eight-year-old boy, chased by my boss, propositioned by a mob guy, strangled by a husband, and avoided a serial killer by the skin of my teeth. And the thing is, these events are nothing compared to the experiences of many women who have survived much, *much* more."

The advice columnist walked across the bridge, stepped into her yard, put Vagina T. down on the picnic table, and glanced happily around her little island. Earlier in the year, she had painted the trees blue and hung plastic egg crates from the branches.

"I have met women from Louisiana to Vermont, and I can

tell you one thing," she said. "I never met a damsel. *Never met a damsel!* The ten-thousand–year-old damsel-in-distress story is dead. Bad things still happen to women, yes; but women are no longer damsels. Women are sweaty. Women are scalding. Women are strong. Women are tender. Women are fierce. Women are fighters!"

The advice columnist reached into the hole of a tree, pulled out a bottle of Veuve Clicquot champagne, and popped the cork.

"Ladies!" she shouted. "A toast to the warrioresses!" She paused, turned, saluted, and raised the bottle toward the west. "And to the great state of Montana!" Not stopping to go in the cabin to fetch a glass, the advice columnist drank deep.

Author's Note

On my walk across the Star Mountains of Papua New Guinea with Sali, the son of the Telefomin Big Man, and Bikki, the Atbalman warrior, as my guides and companions, we trekked through vast areas where tribes were at war. I hired "a guard for the body." A second guard for the body was hired to guard the first guard for the body. Both guards for the body carried bows and arrows. There was, however, a problem. Neither guard for the body would agree to guard the body of a woman (i.e., me).

Sali solved the dilemma by telling the two guards of the body that I had been "proclaimed an honorary man."

It worked.

And because it happens that I like certain chaps—I am now proclaiming the following men to be . . .

HONORARY WOMEN

David Quammen	Tom Robbins	Tom Carroll
Steve Byers	David Hirshey	Rob Fleder
Andy Switzer	Jamie Harris	Bobbie Simmons
Tom Van Arsdale	Dick Van Arsdale	Mike Troy
Fred Schmidt	Ed Kosner	Michael Solomon
Jim Morgan	Alex Heard	Terry McDonell
Bill Tonelli	Jim Signorelli	Michael Porte
Jack McDevitt	Gavin Caruthers	Chris Schelling
Greg Talenfeld	Bob Roe	David Yeater
Kenneth Shaw	George Butler	Kyle Fisher
Sali	Bikki	Berry Blanton
Tom Carroll IV	Kenneth Hogan	Mike Tulin

Ladies, if you would like to nominate a person to be an Honorary Woman, please list that person's name on our Official Honorary Women Roll at ejeancarroll.com. I look forward to compiling a glorious and rousing roster!

Acknowledgments

I acknowledge that Nina Garcia is fabulous. I acknowledge that my niece, Lauren Switzer Harris, will one day take over the city of New York. I acknowledge that Robbie Myers is magnificent. I acknowledge that my sisters, Cande Carroll and Barbara Carroll are far superior to me. I acknowledge that Leah Chernikoff is stunning, Lisa Chase is dazzling, Laurie Abraham is sensational and that Emma Rosenblum is super duper. I acknowledge that Eileen Bertelli dragged my withered carcass to the emergency room. I acknowledge that Ginnie McDevitt brought me nuts in the hospital. I acknowledge that Dr. Steve Menlove sent me to Dr. Jeffrey Green who saved what was left of me. I acknowledge that Dr. Kent Sepkowitz's brain is the biggest brain on the Island of Manhattan. I acknowledge that C.C. Dyer, Melanie Rock, Nancy Haas, Susan Squire, Nessa Rapoport, Dodai Stewart, Tiffany Star, Patricia De Paula Moreira, Nancy Logan, Robin Tovey, Nancy Serfas, Tricia Tilton, Ivy Tulin, Bella Tino, Donna Roe, Susan (Hi, Shi Han!) Huang Shaw, Eve Blazo, Julia Armet, Jan Cherubin, Jan Arcangeli, Rebecca Guenther, and Jane Michels are all so brilliant, that brilliant is not the word.

I acknowledge that I hate Facebook. I acknowledge that I loathe Instagram. I acknowledge that I am flogging *What Do We Need Men For* on Facebook and Instagram. I confess that the copyeditors, Sara Ensey and Chris Ensey, deserve induction into the Rock & Roll Hall of Fame. I grant that Susan Walsh is the Elsa Schiaparelli of book designers, that Lisa Davis is the Ida Lupino of production editors, and that Jennifer P. McArdle should be attorney general. I admit that I plan to drink a glass of Chartreuse tonight in honor of Laura Apperson. I admit that after I drink that glass of Chartreuse, I will divulge under no duress whatsoever that Danielle Prielipp is breathtaking and that Dori Weintraub is amazing.

I acknowledge that I raise my hat to Laura Clark, that I doff my wig to Jen Enderlin, that I shout three tremendous hurrahs for Sally Richardson, and that I throw myself at the feet of Jeanette Zwart, Jeff Capshew, and the famous St. Martin's Press sales team and shall remain prostrate there until Pub date.

I acknowledge that the burly-nippled Sarah Lazin is the best of all possible agents living or dead. And, with my hand on my left bra strap, I acknowledge that Elisabeth Dyssegaard is the greatest literary editor of the twenty-first century and that I am sending her a lock of my hair.

AND BOBBING A CURTSEY TO THE LADIES OF THE WHAT DO WE NEED MEN FOR TOWNS:

Elnora, Indiana
Cynthiana, Indiana
Anita, Indiana
Bonnie, Illinois
Ina, Illinois
Marion, Illinois
Anna, Illinois
Pocahontas, Missouri
Blytheville, Arkansas
Marion, Arkansas
Jennette, Arkansas
Marie, Arkansas
Victoria, Arkansas
Marianna, Arkansas

Helena, Arkansas
Ethel, Arkansas
Elaine, Arkansas
Eudora, Arkansas
Tallulah, Louisiana
Pearl, Mississippi
Verona, Mississippi
Florence, Alabama
Bonnieville, Kentucky
Elizabethtown, Kentucky
Marysville, Ohio
Marion, Ohio
Minerva, Ohio
Angelica, New York
Henrietta, New York
Charlotte, Vermont
Eden, Vermont

With a kiss to Vagina T. Fireball and a *Clak Clak Clak* for me,
on April 9, 2018
Lewis Carroll romped off this mortal coil and began the
Greatest of All Road Trips—
Destination: Heaven
(#334 most popular girl's name)